## DATE DUE

| | | | |
|---|---|---|---|
| MAY 3 | | | |
| 2 6 | | | |
| JAN 2 | | | |
| APR 9 | | | |
| SEP 16 '82 | | | |
| | | | |
| | | | |
| | | | |
| | | | |
| | | | |
| | | | |
| | | | |
| | | | |
| | | | |
| | | | |
| | | | |

# ADVENTURES IN FLIGHT

# ON SILENT WINGS

## WINGS

### ADVENTURES IN MOTORLESS FLIGHT

By
Don Dwiggins

GROSSET & DUNLAP, INC.
PUBLISHERS · NEW YORK
A NATIONAL GENERAL COMPANY

To the future soaring pilots of America
who may be moved by this book to share the joy
of soaring on silent wings,
and so learn more about the sky and themselves.

Photo Credits: Don Dwiggins, 3, 4, 6, 7, 13, 22, 29, 54, 56, 96, 98, 123, 126, 135, 136, 138, 139, 144, 145; Karl Brauer, 1, 15, 34, 37, 38, 40, 42, 43, 45, 46, 49, 50; Bob O'Hara, 141; National Air and Space Museum, 10, 14, 16, 18, 21, 26, 30; Alexander Schleicher, 146; United States Air Force, 68, 76, 82, 86, 88, 90–91, 93, 100, 103, 104, 105, 106, 108; Elmer Dyer, 24; California State Library, 28; David Hatfield, 32, 57, 74, 77 top, 80, 84; Ryan Aeronautical Company, 147; Schweizer Aircraft Corporation, 52, 61, 64, 66; Title Insurance and Trust Company, 55; Glenn Bowlus, 58; Los Angeles County Museum, 60; All American Engineering Company, 70; Harold D. Hoekstra, 73, 75; Jack Laister, 77 bottom; Imperial War Museum, 99, 102; University of California at Los Angeles, 110, 112, 118; Environmental Sciences Service Administration (ESSA), 113, 120; Larry Edgar, 114 top; Los Angeles Daily News, 114 bottom, 117; Charles V. Lindsay, 124; Paul Bikle, 129; Bill Ordway, 130; Don Hoster, 132; Dick Johnson, 133.

# CONTENTS

1   WINGS OF THE WIND                     1
2   SECRETS OF THE BIRDS                 19
3   THE BIRDMEN OF HESSE                 33
4   THE AMERICAN WAY                     53
5   WINGS OF WAR                         69
6   THE MOONSET MACHINES                 87
7   TO THE STRATOSPHERE                 111
8   THE SKY SURFERS                     127
    RECOMMENDED READING                 151

The author is indebted to numerous individuals and organizations for the time and effort they have given to help assemble this first detailed account of gliding and soaring in war and peace. Foremost among these are the staffs of the Soaring Society of America; the National Air & Space Museum of the Smithsonian Institution; the United States Air Forces Historical Division's Research Studies Institute; the Research Library of the University of California at Los Angeles; the Imperial War Museum of London; and the private collections of David D. Hatfield, Northrop Institute of Technology; of Mr. Karl Brauer; and of the Title Insurance & Trust Company.

Among the many individuals who helped in this project are Paul Bikle, Glenn Bowlus, Helen Dick, A. Felix du Pont, Jr., Lieutenant Colonel Phil W. Garrison, Harold D. Hoekstra, William Ivans, Richard H. Johnson, Jack Laister, Charles V. Lindsay, Hannes Linke, Tom McBride, George Michanowsky, William Ordway, Fred Robinson, Ernest W. Robischon, Paul Schweizer, Floyd J. Sweet, Mrs. Eleanor Velarde, and Thomas J. Winkler, Sr. Special thanks go also to Barbara Zahler, whose editorial guidance and forbearance were invaluable.

# ON SILENT WINGS

Otto Lilienthal launched from his "jumping off place"—a tower built atop a 45-foot man-made hill.

# 1/WINGS OF THE WIND

*"Had man been intended to fly, God would have
given him wings."*
William Cowper, 1783.

THE ART OF SOARING FLIGHT, long the special province of the birds, today
is enjoyed by thousands of young men and women who consider it one of
the most challenging and rewarding of all aerial activities. Relating to
powered flight as sailboating does to power-boating, riding on invisible
atmospheric currents brings a special joy to the pilot, who draws upon the
energies of the sky itself in order to stay aloft. The carefree soaring enthu-
siast, whispering quietly along a mountain ridge into the teeth of a slope
wind, or spiraling his lonely way inside a rising thermal bubble, is one
with the eagle wheeling through space on silent wings. His mount, a high
performance sailplane, is a thing of sheer beauty, its slender, symmetric
design the embodiment of architect Frank Lloyd Wright's dictum that "form
follows function." It is the realization of a dream man held for centuries, to
ride on wings of the wind.

As recently as 1908, Sir Hiram Maxim, a pioneer of heavier-than-air
flight, wrote: "We shall never be able to imitate the flight of soaring birds.
We cannot hope to make a sensitive apparatus that will work quick enough
to take advantage of the rising columns of air, and he who seeks to fly has
this problem to deal with."

Early aircraft designers who sought to translate the mystery of flight into
practical terms had a choice of two designs—the ornithopter (wing-flapper)
and the rigid wing. As yet, no ornithopter has flapped its wings as efficiently
as a bird, and only recently have sailplane designers proven Sir Hiram
wrong.

Tales abound of men who jumped off high places with artificial wings to
achieve bird flight; they reveal how far back in antiquity man sought to
give wings to his imagination. There was the legendary Chinese Emperor
Shun, said to have been taught to fly by two lovely maidens four thousand
years ago . . . the myths of Daedalus and Icarus, of Abaris, and Archytas
. . . of King Bladud, father of King Lear . . . of Simon the Magician, a
performer of 67 A.D.

1

In mid-nineteenth century, a French librarian, Louis Nicolas Bescherelle, related the legend of Oliver, The Wizard of Malmsbury, a Benedictine monk: "Having manufactured some wings . . . and having fastened them to his hands, he sprang from the top of a tower against the wind. He succeeded in sailing a distance of 125 paces; but either through the impetuous whirling of the wind, or through nervousness resulting from his audacious enterprise, he fell to the earth and broke his legs. Henceforth he dragged a miserable, languishing existence [he died in 1060], attributing his misfortune to having failed to attach a tail to his feet."

Another adventurer far ahead of his time was an unnamed Saracen, who, according to Bescherelle, leaped from the Hippodrome tower in Constantinople in 1178: "He stood upright, clothed in a white robe, very long and very wide, whose folds, stiffened by willow wands, were to serve as sails to receive the wind. All the spectators kept their eyes intently fixed upon him, and many cried, 'Fly! Fly! O Saracen!' " The Saracen finally got up nerve, and "kept extending his arms to catch the wind. At last, when he deemed it favorable, he rose into the air like a bird; but his flight was as unfortunate as that of Icarus, for the weight of his body having more power to draw him downward than his artificial wings had to sustain him, he fell and broke his bones, and such was his misfortune that instead of sympathy there was only merriment over his misadventure."

A pratfall is a pratfall and got laughs even in the twelfth century, but despite such ridicule, men continued to ponder the mystery of bird flight. It is worth noting that most inventors who attempted flight with homemade wings lived in warm climates, where they had a better opportunity to observe the ways of soaring birds.

Charles Darwin wrote, in his *Voyage of the Beagle:* "When the condors are wheeling in a flock round and round any spot, their flight is beautiful. Except when rising from the ground, I do not remember ever having seen one of these birds flap its wings." It seemed simple enough that birds could propel themselves in such a manner; the mystery was how they could stay up for hours without moving a feather. The idea was born that a mysterious pulsing force existed within the wind itself, waiting to be tapped.

Israel Lancaster, a Chicago inventor, described in the *American Naturalist* of September, 1891, how a 110-pound model glider escaped him in a high wind in Colorado, drawn forcibly from his hands by something he called "aspiration." Professor Samuel P. Langley, secretary of the Smithsonian Institution, was led by experimentation to conclude that soaring birds

2

History and legend abound with tales of men who sought to "ride on wings of the wind."
Above is Retif de la Bretone's *Flying Man*.

drew energy from a vibratory or oscillating movement of the air, which he described in his treatise, *The Internal Work of the Wind.*

Even the great Leonardo da Vinci saw magical properties in bird flight, in the sixteenth century, after defining some basic aerodynamic principles. Two centuries before Sir Isaac Newton, Leonardo wrote: "The movement of the air against a fixed thing is as great as the movement of the movable thing against the air which is immovable." Da Vinci also noted that birds often soared along ridges where slope winds blew; he called these *reflex winds.* In his later work can be found sketches showing graceful bird wings impinging on lines of relative airflow. He had come close to understanding the mystery of soaring, but instead of using this knowledge to construct a

In the sixteenth century, Leonardo da Vinci came close to understanding the mystery of soaring, but instead of using his knowledge to construct a workable glider, he used his theories of flight to explain such events as creation, life, and the end of the world.

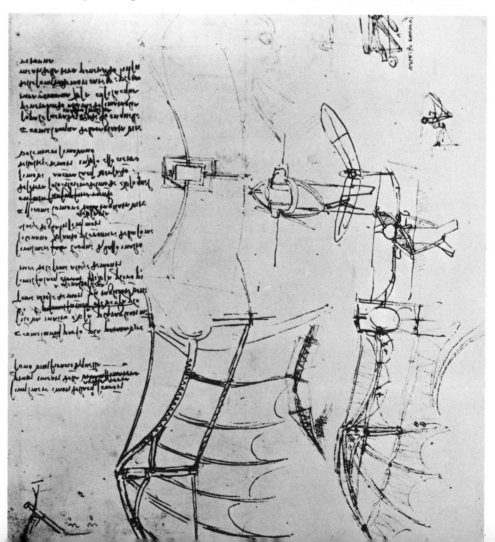

workable glider, he included drawings among his famous Deluge sketches, seeking with them to explain such events as creation, life, and the end of the world. In linking flight and cosmology, he lifted the natural laws of aerodynamics to a metaphysical plane.

At the beginning of this century, Sir Hiram Maxim observed: "Man is essentially a land animal, and it is quite possible if Nature had not placed before him numerous examples of birds and insects that are able to fly, he would never have thought of attempting it himself." A nineteenth century French sea captain, Jean Marie le Bris, was inspired by the flight of the albatross, a bird that effortlessly followed the fastest sailing ships rounding Cape Horn. Le Bris shot one to learn its secret and dramatically wrote: "I took the wing and exposed it to the breeze; and lo! in spite of me it drew forward into the wind; notwithstanding my resistance it tended to rise. Thus I had discovered the secret of the bird! I comprehended the whole mystery of flight!"

The legend persists that in the 1840's le Bris built a large wood-and-fabric albatross with 50-foot wingspread and launched it from a horse-drawn wagon on a country road near Douarnenez, France. It rose to a height of 300 feet, at the end of a tether rope. According to the story, the rope tangled around the body of the driver, jerking him aloft, howling in fright and anguish, until le Bris came down. He is said to have flown a second mechanical albatross from a quay at Brest, covering two dozen yards before alighting. Unfortunately, the feats of le Bris remain legendary when one checks the source: Octave Chanute's *Progress in Flying Machines,* published in Chicago, in 1894. Chanute admitted in a footnote he borrowed the story from a romantic novel, *Les Grandes Amours,* written in 1878 by the French author, G. de la Landelle, and included it only because le Bris, like Lancaster and himself, apparently believed in "aspiration."

Orville Wright, who with his brother Wilbur pioneered slope soaring in 1902, snorted: "The stories of the experiments of Jean Marie le Bris are too absurd to be given any serious consideration; it is impossible to perform any of the feats attributed to him with a structure such as he used."

In their subsequent struggle to go unchallenged as the true "fathers of flight," Orville and Wilbur Wright questioned the claims of Gustave Whitehead, a German-born Bridgeport, Connecticut, engineer who worked in the Locomobile factory and moonlighted as an airplane inventor. Yet more than two years before the Wrights' first powered flights at Kitty Hawk, the

Bridgeport *Herald* reported on August 18, 1901, that Whitehead's birdlike monoplane carried him half a mile, in a dawn flight on the 14th; the New York *Herald* and the Boston *Transcript* also ran the story. A photograph of Whitehead aloft in a triplane glider was published in the *Scientific American* on September 19, 1903—still three months before Kitty Hawk. Scoffed Orville: "The Whitehead story is too incredible and ridiculous to require serious refutation."

If the Wrights were quick to discredit rival glider men, they were lenient with Sir George Cayley, a British inventor who built and flew model gliders a century before them. "[Sir George] knew more of the principles of aeronautics than any of his predecessors, and as much as any that followed him up to the end of the nineteenth century," Orville asserted.

Picking up where da Vinci left off, Sir George had gone about aerial experimentation scientifically, using wing dihedral and a tailplane on an 1804 model to achieve lateral and longitudinal stability. "It was very pretty to see it sail down a steep hill," he wrote. "It gave the idea that a large instrument would be a better and safer conveyance down the Alps than even a sure-footed mule!" Subsequently Sir George built bigger gliders and launched them from a hill behind his home at Brompton Hall, near Scarborough, on the North Coast of England. During one such experiment in 1809, Sir George's coachman, like le Bris', is said to have accidentally glided 300 yards across a ravine.

The Wright brothers scoffed at reports that a glider, built in 1840 by French sea captain Jean Marie le Bris, ever flew.

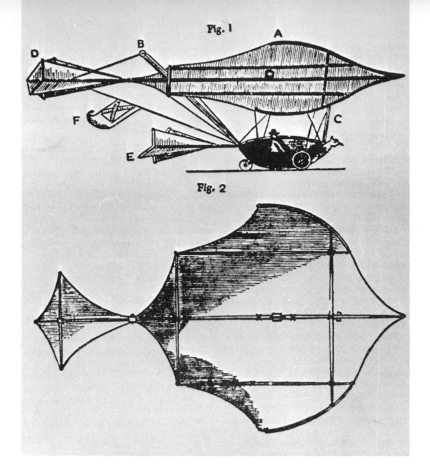

Sketch of Sir George Cayley's 1852 glider model.

Glider development in the United States followed a casual pattern until the last decade of the nineteenth century; flying machine inventors were considered irresponsible nuts like those who tinkered with perpetual motion machines. Typical was Melville M. Murrell, who labored on his inventions in his father's barn at Panther Springs, Tennessee, on the Knoxville-to-Bristol coach road. Melville had always entertained a desire to fly; in 1877, at the age of twenty-two, he won a United States patent for an "Improvement in Aerial Navigators" of the ornithopter type. Unable to get the thing off the ground, he redesigned it as a rigid wing monoplane, with horizontal tail surface and pivoted side vanes for steering. According to family records, he did make several short glides over his father's apple orchard, at the end of a tow rope. Murrell finally abandoned inventing to become a circuit rider; he carried the word of God to backwoods communities for 45 years, leaving flight up to the birds.

The graceful flight of condors wheeling against the cloud-flecked skies of Colorado inspired another forgotten inventor of the period. Ever since running away from home in St. Louis in 1842, as a boy of fifteen, to fight in the Mexican War, Reuben Jasper Spalding, a prospector of Rosita, Colorado, had longed to soar with the big birds floating so easily along craggy ridges. For 17 years he labored on a lovely spread of wings, behind closed doors in his smoke-filled blacksmith shop; the bewhiskered miner was a ripe sixty-three by the time he considered the wings ready for a tryout. Word of the flying machine leaked out when William J. Orange, enterprising editor of the *Silver Creek Russler,* sneaked into Spalding's barn one day in 1890 and wrote a feature story about what he saw:

"The machine is fashioned exactly like a bird's wings and tail. These and all the springs, hinges, cords, and devices to operate them are attached to a leather harness. The steel used is of the best quality, having cost 80 cents a pound. Fourteen feathers sprout from each wing, fashioned from silk and eagle quills. There is a head rest and leg rests and the flapping, curving and folding of the wings is controlled by an easy forward arm motion." The Patent Commissioner, according to Orange, considered it "the only perfect duplicate of nature's flying apparatus ever made in the world." Patent Number 398,984 was duly issued to Spalding on March 5, 1889.

Spalding caused considerable comment on this trip to Washington to see the Patent Office people, with his model tucked underneath his arm. Back home, he announced finally that a public flight demonstration would be

In this 1877 glider, Melville M. Murrell is said to have made several glides over his family's apple orchard.

made in Denver. Shops were closed, classes dismissed. Cowhands and miners gathered to see a man fly. Reuben strapped on his wings and proudly jogged up and down the street a few times to limber up, his grandson, Clarence Spalding, remembers. "Go ahead and fly!" someone jeered. A gun went off; dust exploded at his feet. In alarm, Spalding ran for the courthouse, wings flapping with each leap. He didn't quite get off the ground; he hadn't meant to—not that way. He was waiting for friends to arrive with a hot-air circus balloon to lift him into the sky, so he could glide back to earth.

The cowpokes, feeling their liquor, ran after the frightened old man, grabbed him bodily and tossed him high in the air, amid shouts of laughter. But Spalding was tough. He lit into the crowd like an avenging angel, kicking and punching. When the dust settled his lovely wings were smashed, the leather harness bearing the slashes of sharp Bowie knives. "I saw those knife cuts after they had been neatly repaired by my grandfather," the grandson said.

Public ridicule dismayed the old man. He sadly packed away his angel wings and forgot about flying, and died at Swallows, Colorado, April 19, 1902. The wings were destroyed by fire in 1917, but two patent models exist to show what the old man's dreams were made of. One reposes in the National Air and Space Museum in Washington, a tribute to a western pioneer who had done his best to fly like a bird. The other was given to the author.

On September 24, 1892, the United States Patent Officer heard from Louis Pierre Mouillard, a French engineer living in Cairo, Egypt, who discovered, from watching the flight of vultures, a hitherto unrecognized principle of equilibrium—how a bird changes its wing shape to make a turn. The patent was the first granted for ailerons, which Mouillard patterned after the vulture's tip feathers.

"Observation confers knowledge," Mouillard wrote. "It is first important to see, and then to understand." He spent long hours at his observation post, studying the flight of the great tawny African vulture. "Big as a sheep, weighing 16 pounds, his majestic sailing on rigid wings seems the perfection of simplicity . . . he sweeps in circles and he rises high . . . the peculiarity is that he expends no force, either to sustain or to guide himself. He detests flapping; of all birds he decomposes the forces of the wind, and utilizes them with the greatest skill. . . ."

9

The patent model of Reuben Jasper Spalding's gliding machine (above) is now in the Smithsonian. Bottom, is the rear view of the machine showing tail feathers.

Mouillard was one of a number of aerial experimenters who submitted scientific papers to history's fist Congress on Aerial Navigation, held at the Chicago World's Fair in 1893. Octave Chanute was chairman. A good number of delegates made this an historic meeting, establishing that man was on the brink of achieving successful powered flight. Yet there was a scattering of cranks, one of whom suddenly rushed to the podium and shouldered Chanute aside, waving a paper on "Negative Gravity." Chanute winced—if read, the paper would go into the minutes of the meeting, for posterity to laugh at. There was enough to do keeping the meeting serious, with folks clamoring outside to hear John Phillip Sousa's Marine Band, ride the first giant Ferris wheel, and admire a torso-twisting belly dancer named Little Egypt. The intruder, dressed gaudily in tight checkered pants, red vest, swallowtail coat and starched collar, cleared his throat and began to read loudly:

"One point I have studied, and that is, how can a 20-pound wild goose carry itself so easily? Weigh every feather you can pick off from a wild goose, and they will not weigh one pound! Now if the feathers be picked off from the goose he can come no nearer to flying than we can!"

A shocked murmur ran through the audience as he continued: "So there we have it clearly demonstrated, that one pound of goose feathers can pick up 19 pounds of goose and carry this 19 pounds and its one pound of feathers through space at about half a mile a minute, if in a hurry.

"Now, my theory is this—and it applies to all birds. Notice any bird when he suddenly starts to fly, and you will notice a lightning-like quiver of his feathers. I believe that this quiver causes the production of a negative force of magnetism, or some kind of force which pushes the bird from earth—just the reverse of the lodestone.

"He then has only to use his wings to propel the body, for the magnetic negative earth-force does the lifting, and that is produced by the feathers. If it were not, then the bird ought to fly when divested of his feathers. This is the force which should be looked for! Whoever discovers it will make a fortune!"

One of the more remarkable glider flights of the 1890's is worthy of mention only because it never took place—it existed in the imagination of a brilliant German hunchback, Charles Steinmetz, whose fellow socialist students gave him the nickname *Proteus* during his university days at Breslau. Steinmetz joined the General Electric Company in Schenectady, New York, in 1893, the year that Octave Chanute was hosting flying machine inventors at Chicago. Possessed of a vast knowledge of mathematics, Steinmetz published a 200-page explanation of the theory of alternating current.

After reading the Chicago aeronautical reports, he was prompted in the winter of 1894–95 to form a group to solve the mystery of flight—it seemed simple compared to knotty electrical problems he'd come to grips with. Thus was born the world's first gliding club—the Mohawk Aerial Navigation and Exploration Company, Unlimited. In the summer of 1895 the club members carried their first glider out to the Rotterdam Hills, five miles from Schenectády. Little more than a pair of hinged canvas wings attached to a framework, they were, to say the least, unsatisfactory. Steinmetz puffed on a cigar and frowned as one member after another sprinted down hill, flapping the wings like a wounded butterfly. Unless success were attained, the association would soon be without members. Quietly, he sneaked a folding camera from his coat pocket, and snapped a picture of one club member poised for "takeoff." Back at his laboratory, he developed the negative and carefully retouched it; where the grassy hillside sloped away now appeared open sky, trees, and rooftops.

At the next meeting Steinmetz displayed the retouched photo. The effect was generally electric. The Steinmetz machine really worked—old Proteus had a picture to prove it! His darkroom magic achieved the hoped for results; it provided a good laugh and stimulated the group to press on. By 1895 they'd tried three different models, and only then gave up when one member, engaged to be married, nearly broke his neck when he tripped and somersaulted trying to get off the ground. If Steinmetz did not solve the mystery of flight, he at least added an amusing episode to the story of gliding, with a hoax still talked about in upstate New York.

European glider builders were having better success in the 1890's than their American peers. In 1891 the good burghers of Berlin, Germany, were startled to see a stocky, middle-aged man of forty-three cavorting about his backyard flapping a pair of fabric wings. Peering over the fence, they watched him bend forward and run hard for a score of steps, plunge onto a wooden springboard and propel himself into the air. His feet kicking, he hung suspended, frantically trying to maintain balance before tumbling down.

Otto Lilienthal was a mechanical engineer and member of the German Society for the Advancement of Aerial Navigation, who, with his brother

Charles Proteus Steinmetz, wizard of electricity at General Electric in Schenectady, New York, turned to gliding in 1894, and formed the world's first gliding club, Mohawk Aerial Navigation & Exploration Company. The only trouble was, the Mohawk glider couldn't get off the ground (above), so Steinmetz made it "fly" in his darkroom by touching out the hill, and adding trees and sky!

Gustav, pioneered gliding flight on a scientific basis with considerable success. For a quarter century they systematically analyzed the problem of bird flight, and came to the conclusion that skillful use of curved wings and a good breeze were all they needed to fly.

Once Otto had learned to manage his wings, he took them out to the country, found a hill sloping into a steady wind and there achieved glides of more than 80 feet. Encouraged, he spent the winter designing new wings with better balance. Weighing 53 pounds, they contained 172 square feet of surface, with his weight loaded to 1.33 lbs. per square foot. Happily, Otto invited out a friend, Herr Krassner, of the Berlin Meteorological Institute, who photographed him "sailing right over the head of the miller of Derwitz (in whose barn I stored my apparatus) and of his esteemed poodle dog."

Lilienthal shrewdly avoided the myth that mysterious forces in the wind held the secret of soaring: "When we look at the safe and quiet sailing of the birds, it almost seems as if some undiscovered mechanical principle were at work, some feature in the elastic properties of air, or in the elastic curvature of the feathers, which accounts for the mystery of sailing flight; but my experiments have taught me there is no mystery. Dexterity alone invests the native inhabitants of the air with superiority over man in that element." He became obsessed with the idea that with practice he could duplicate a bird's dexterity. It was an obsession that would drive him to accomplish more than 2,000 glides, and eventually crash to his death.

By 1893 Otto had sailed more than 100 yards at an altitude of 75 feet in one minute; with favorable winds he extended that record to more than 400 yards. The winds were not always right, so he had built a conical hill 50 feet high; from its summit he could glide in any direction from whence

Burghers of Germany watch as Otto Lilienthal makes a glide. Lilienthal had to swing his legs like a gymnast to keep the glider wings level.

In 1895, Lilienthal built and flew a graceful biplane glider in which he included enough wing area to sustain a motor.

the wind blew. Gripping the framework of his graceful wings, he would leap from the hillside, tuck his legs up and go sky-sliding, swinging his legs first to one side and then the other like a gymnast to maintain balance. For a man close to fifty, he was having the time of his life. He stretched his glides to more than a quarter mile, from the summit of a ridge in the Rhinow Hills; as his fame spread over Europe families packed picnic lunches to come and watch.

Whiskers blowing, eyes afire, Otto out-distanced the children who raced after him listening for the odd drumming sound of wind thrumming over taut wire braces. After each flight, eager hands helped him haul his bird machine back uphill. By 1895 Lilienthal was flying a graceful biplane glider in which he included enough wing area to sustain a motor. He had no interest in inventing an airplane; he simply wanted a powered glider to fly when the winds were down. He was getting along in years. The strain of running hard to get a launch was proving too much for him.

In 1896 Otto returned to the monoplane design, with a control system operated by simply moving his head. It was his dream to fly through a full 360-degree turn—gliding straight ahead was no better than tobogganing. He confided to his diary: "I have made up my mind, by means of either a stronger wind or by flapping wings, to get higher up and further away from the hills, so that sailing round in circles, I can follow the strong up-lifting currents and have sufficient airspace under and around me to com-

15

plete with safety a circle, and lastly, to come up against the wind again to land."

With this goal in mind he set off on August 11, 1896, from a hill near the village of Rhinow in the evening after most of the day's visitors had departed. His mechanic, Hugo Eulitz, helped him into his machine, then watched him go loping downhill into the wind. A sudden gust caught a wing, sweeping him sharply upward. Eulitz cried out as the craft hung motionless, then plunged to earth in a spiraling dive. There was a sickening thud; Otto Lilienthal lay still, his spine broken.

The Wright brothers could not ignore Otto Lilienthal's scientific approach to gliding flight. A few days before his own fatal illness, Wilbur would publicly denigrate the old German, in a letter to the Aero Club of America: "The question arises as to whether or not [Lilienthal] would have solved the problem of human flight if his untimely death in 1896 had not interrupted his efforts. . . . His methods of controlling balance, both laterally and longitudinally, were exceedingly crude and quite insufficient. Although he experimented for six successive years, 1891–1896, with gliding machines, he was using at the end of the same inadequate method of control with which he started."

Otto Lilienthal's death ended the career of the first true birdman, but photographs of his machines in flight inspired others to carry on his work. In England, Percy Sinclair Pilcher, a marine engineer, built a series of four

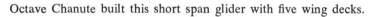

Octave Chanute built this short span glider with five wing decks.

Lilienthal type gliders in 1895–96—the *Bat,* the *Beetle,* the *Gull,* and the *Hawk.* Things went well, and Pilcher was on the eve of installing a small engine in a fifth machine when he decided to amuse some friends by making a flight in the *Hawk* on September 30, 1899, an inauspiciously windy day. Launched at the end of a rope wound around a winch, the *Hawk* suddenly zoomed skyward when struck by a strong gust, as had Lilienthal's glider. A stay wire snapped, a wing buckled and Pilcher crashed to his death.

In America, Octave Chanute, who had helped organize the Conference on Aerial Navigation at Chicago and had compiled the world's existing knowledge of aeronautics in his book, *Progress in Flying Machines,* in 1896 took a hand at building gliders himself. Using engineering data, rather than copying the wing of a bird, Chanute, a bridge-builder, designed a rigid biplane as he would design a steel truss. Remarkably light and strong, it was braced with compression struts and tension wires, all mathematically correct. Chanute took his glider to Dune Park, a sandy region near Gary, Indiana, but at sixty-four considered himself too old to risk flying himself. Two assistants, A.M. Herring and William Avery, did the gliding.

The Chanute biplane glider actually was the result of considerable trial-and-error experimentation with other forms of wing arrangements. The first was of the Lilienthal monoplane type, the second had six decks of wings; neither was successful, and gradually he reduced the number of decks to two. The biplane glider carried 135 square feet of curved canvas, weighed only 23 pounds and could support a 180-pound man in flight. More than 2,000 successful flights were made with Chanute gliders at Dune Park, some reaching 360 feet. Chanute's daughter, Elizabeth, wrote to the author: "You are correct that my father did not make gliding flights himself. I believe he did just once, but he did not tell us of it until some time much later, as he had promised my mother he would not take the risk of breaking any bones, at his age. . . ."

Unlike the Wright brothers, who jealously guarded their ideas, Chanute was one of aviation's great patrons, giving freely both advice and money to young inventors who came to him for help. Even the Wrights were moved to admit that "If Chanute had not lived, the entire history of progress in flying would have been other than it has been."

Following Chanute's death, on November 23, 1910, the Aero Club of Washington memorialized him along with Otto Lilienthal, Samuel P. Langley, and Sir Hiram Maxim, as men who did most to develop flying before Kitty Hawk: "These four men elevated an inquiry, which for years had been classed with such absurdities as perpetual motion and squaring of the circle, to the dignity of a legitimate engineering pursuit. . . ."

In 1905, tandem glider designer John J. Montgomery barnstormed with an aerial troupe of glider pilots and stunt men.

# 2/THE SECRET OF THE BIRDS

To understand something of the miracle of flight, one has only to walk along a wind-swept beach and observe the evolutions of gulls diving, climbing, wheeling, sometimes soaring with wings extended, at other times sharply swiveling wing and tail, virtually stopping in midair, to pounce on a bit of food, or alight on a wave, yet never falling, never out of positive control.

At the turn of the century, Wilbur and Orville Wright, of Dayton, Ohio, began spending long hours studying the miracle of how different species of birds maneuver. Wilbur noted anything unusual in his notebook, and from those notes they sought to learn where Lilienthal, Chanute, and others had failed to master *controllability,* which they considered the secret of true flight. In his tight scrawl, Wilbur noted:

· The buzzard, which uses the dihedral angle, finds greater difficulty to maintain equilibrium in strong winds than eagles and hawks which hold their wings level.

· The hen hawk can rise faster than the buzzard and its motion is steadier. It displays less effort in maintaining balance.

· Hawks are better soarers than buzzards but more often resort to flapping because they wish greater speed.

· A damp day is unfavorable for soaring unless there is a high wind.

· No bird soars in a calm.

· All soarers, but especially the buzzard, seem to keep their fore and aft balance more by shifting the center of resistance than by shifting the center of lift.

In 1900 the Wrights established a base of bird study at Kill Devil Hill, a sloping sand dune near Kitty Hawk, North Carolina, behind a wide beach over which sea breezes blew steadily. There, "bald eagles, ospreys, hawks and buzzards gave us daily exhibitions of their powers. The buzzards were the most numerous and were the most persistent soarers. They apparently never flapped except when absolutely necessary, while the eagles and hawks usually soared only when they were at leisure."

Their bird lore grew: "When the weather was cold and damp and the wind strong, the buzzards would be seen soaring back and forth along the hills or at the edge of a clump of trees. They were evidently taking advantage of the current of air flowing upward over these obstructions. On such days they were often utterly unable to soar except in these special places. But on warm, clear days when the wind was light, they would be seen high in the air, soaring in great circles. Usually it seemed necessary for them to reach a height of several hundred feet by flapping before this style of soaring became possible."

With such observations they discovered the different kinds of air on which soaring birds rode—strong, sometimes gusty slope winds that ruffled across sand dunes, and thermal bubbles that rose invisibly high into blue skies whenever Kill Devil Hill baked hot beneath a summer sun.

Sometimes they watched great numbers of shore birds circling in one spot, "rising together higher and higher, till finally they would disperse, each gliding off in whatever direction it wished to go. At such times other buzzards, only a short distance away, found it necessary to flap frequently, but when they reached a point beneath the circling flock, they too began to rise on motionless wings."

One day Wilbur noted a curious thing, as two bald eagles circled round and round, hunting thermal lift. "After a time, our attention was attracted to the flashing of some object considerably lower down. Examination with a field glass proved it to be a feather, which one of the birds had evidently cast. Soon it was no longer falling, but on the contrary, was rising rapidly. It finally went out of sight upward, drawn into the same rising current in which the eagles were soaring."

On other days, when the winds blew strong across Albermarle Sound, "the birds were compelled to make use of the currents flowing up the sides of the hills, and it was possible for us to measure the velocity and trend of the wind in which the soaring was performed." One day they watched a flight of four buzzards soaring along the northeast slope of the hill; their wings, Wilbur noted, met the wind inclined about five degrees above the horizon.

"There is no question in my mind," Wilbur concluded, "that men can build wings having as little or less relative resistance than that of the best soaring birds. The bird's wings were undoubtedly very well designed indeed, but it is not any extraordinary efficiency that strikes with astonishment, but rather the marvelous skill with which they are used."

Their first glider wings incorporated the Chanute double-deck design, though they felt a tail was both unnecessary and troublesome. In its place they added a small canard elevator surface in front, "in such a position that the action of the wind upon it would counterbalance the effect of the travel of the center of pressure on the main surface." Their grasp of a wing's dynamics was a virtual breakthrough. Wrote Wilbur: "The amount of lift is of less relative importance than the ratio of lift to drift (drag), as this alone decides the angle of the gliding descent." Today, sailplane designers adhere to this formula in seeking the highest L/D ratio for maximum performance.

In the summer of 1900 the Wrights flew their biplane glider as a kite at Kitty Hawk, with one brother or the other lying on the bottom wing. In a wind of 25 mph the machine lifted, but it flew at a too-steep angle of attack of nearly 20 degrees. They balanced by twisting the wingtips much as a bird does, instead of shifting their weight like Lilienthal and Chanute. When they felt ready to attempt actual gliding, they carried their craft four miles south of Kitty Hawk to Kill Devil Hill. There, true controlled manflight was born, on a 100-foot high sand dune sloping toward the northeast into a strong, gusty wind. "As we had no experience at all in gliding," wrote

The Wright brothers' 1902 glider was a simple Chanute-type biplane with canard front elevator surface and rear rudder. The pilot flew from a prone position.

Orville Wright soared for nine minutes 45 seconds in a slope wind at Kitty Hawk in 1911. His record stood for a full decade.

Wilbur, "we deemed it unsafe to attempt to leave the ground, but on the day following, the wind having subsided to 14 mph, we made about a dozen glides."

They had hoped to log many hours of gliding practice, but their actual flight time that session totaled less than two minutes. Nonetheless, "setting out as we did, with almost revolutionary theories on many points, and an entirely untried form of machine," wrote Wilbur, "we considered it quite a point to be able to return without having our pet theories completely knocked on the head by the hard logic of experience, and our own brains dashed out in the bargain!"

The following year they returned to Kill Devil Hill with a larger glider, its wing area nearly doubled from 165 to 308 square feet. Octave Chanute came down from Chicago to spend a week and offer what advice he could. On their first flights in 1901 the machine dove to the ground on each launch. Repeatedly, the operator inched farther back to shift the center of gravity, until stable glides of 300 feet were achieved, and yet the brothers were disappointed; full up-elevator was necessary to keep the glider in trim.

During one practice flight, Wilbur was horrified to feel the glider pitch up at a steep angle and hang nearly motionless, the same position from which Lilienthal had stalled and crashed to his death. In alarm he lowered the front elevator and scrambled forward; the machine finally mushed to earth in one piece. Puzzled, the Wrights removed the top wing of their glider and flew it as a monoplane kite, checking the pull on the tether rope at different angles of attack. It finally occurred to them what was happening —at a high angle, the center of pressure moved too far rearward of the center of gravity. To correct the problem, they trussed the wing ribs more tightly, reducing its camber to more nearly that of the 1900 wing. "The machine, with its new curvature, never failed to respond promptly to even small movements of the elevator," Wilbur wrote. "The pilot could cause it to almost skim the ground, following the undulations of the surface, or he could cause it to sail out almost on a level with the starting point, and, passing high above the foot of the hill, gradually settle to the ground."

These low, skimming flights were safer than high glides for gaining experience, the Wrights decided: "Often a glide of several hundred feet would be made at a height of a few feet, or even a few inches. While the high flights were more spectacular, the low ones were fully as valuable for training purposes."

Gradually they mastered the new art, gaining confidence with each glide. Late in the summer of 1902 they decided to attempt true soaring flight on slope winds blowing over a dune they called Little Hill. In the final six days of their stay that year, they made more than 375 flights, sometimes hovering five to six feet above the ground for as long as 15 seconds. At this point they might have gone on to perfect the art of soaring, but their goal was to build and fly a powered aircraft. Thus, on December 17, 1903, they were already veteran glider pilots when they first chugged aloft to make airplane history.

The thrill of soaring was not forgotton by Orville; in 1911 he returned to Kitty Hawk to glide with an automatic stabilizing device. Launching into winds of up to 40 mph, Orville stayed aloft in true soaring flight for more than five minutes at a time. On October 24 he soared 9 minutes 45 seconds, an astonishing record unbeaten for a full decade—a decade in which airplanes would go to war and men would use them in bloody aerial combat.

The Wright brothers were not alone in building and flying gliders in

Movie stunt flyer Paul Mantz flying a replica of Professor Montgomery's 1905 tandem glider, *Santa Clara,* for a scene in the movie "Gallant Journey."

America during the 1900's, although they were the most successful. There were crackpots and cranks, seeking patent rights for weird-looking bird machines that flew only in their imaginations, and there were the serious scientists, like Dr. Alexander Graham Bell, inventor of the telephone. Dr. Bell was a close friend of Professor Samuel Pierpont Langley, secretary of the Smithsonian Institution who brought public ridicule on his head by failing to successfully launch a man-carrying tandem warplane, *Aerodrome No. 1,* from a catapult atop a houseboat anchored in the Potomac River, a few short weeks before the Wrights first flew their aerial gas buggy at Kitty Hawk. Langley, however, had successfully flown a number of large steam-powered models over the Potomac in the 1890's to develop his design, and Dr. Bell was there with a box camera to record the flights.

In 1905 Dr. Bell decided to build his own flying machine, a monster cellular kite with an engine in it. A Hammondsport, New York, motorcycle engine builder, Glenn Curtiss, provided the powerplant. The device was a dismal failure as an aircraft, though it did carry a man aloft when flown as a kite. He was Army Lieutenant Thomas Selfridge, one of a non-profit group organized by Dr. Bell as the Aerial Experiment Association, on September 30, 1907. Selfridge rode the contraption, called the *Cygnet I,* to a height of 168 feet, towed behind a motor launch, but complained that it was about as controllable as a billboard.

Acting on Selfridge's complaint, the AEA next built a biplane glider at the Curtiss plant in Hammondsport, where steady slope winds prevailed. Repeated flights were made by running downhill into a 15-mile breeze. More often than not the glides ended in crashes, until little was left of the machine. The AEA once more changed their goal, this time turning to powered aircraft.

It was in the AEA's first airplane, the *June Bug,* that Glenn Curtiss first experienced the surging power of air in motion, on a July, 1908 flight over Stony Brook Farm near Hammondsport. Unnerved, Curtiss quickly shut off the engine and landed, but soon was back in the air, determinedly searching out the very current he had feared would upset him. This time the *June Bug* was swept up to an altitude of 80 feet, from where he set off on the longest flight yet made by an AEA member.

On October 31, 1911, one week after Orville Wright set his amazing world soaring record of 9¾ minutes, John J. Montgomery, an enigmatic California inventor who claimed to have glided 600 feet down a hill near San Diego 28 years earlier, was killed in the crash of a monoplane glider of his own design at the Ramona Ranch near San Jose.

A controversy still rages over the validity of Montgomery's claims, dating back to efforts of Orville Wright to discredit him during patent litigation with Montgomery heirs. The Wrights, obsessed with their proprietary claim for invention of the three-torque control system, refused to accept that Montgomery's wing warping arrangement for lateral control was invented 20 years before theirs, as the Californian claimed. Wrote Orville in 1944: "Investigation reveals that no invention of Montgomery's is used in airplanes today; no theory originating with his has withstood the test of time. Montgomery's work contributed nothing to the art of flying."

In April, 1911, however, Montgomery spoke before the Aeronautic Society, forerunner of the Aero Club of America, in defense of his claim to have invented wing warping in 1883. Although quite primitive, the machine, patterned after a gull, appears to have been capable of flight, carrying 90 square feet of wing surface and weighing only 38 pounds. Said Montgomery: "I took this apparatus to the top of a hill, facing a gentle

There goes Dan Maloney riding Montgomery's glider slung beneath a hot air balloon at the Santa Clara Fair Grounds, 1905. Maloney was killed shortly after this photo was made.

wind. There was a little run and a jump and I found myself launched into the air. I proceeded against the wind, gliding downhill for a distance of about 600 feet. In this experience I was able to direct my course at will. Wing warping was born at this moment; the machine had great power because I blindly followed the surface provided by nature. . . . I went to nature to study the principle of control. I watched the movements of the vultures and detected in their actions the twisting of the wing. That gave me the solution."

A stout defender of Montgomery was Chanute, to whom he had submitted a paper at the 1893 Chicago Conference on Aerial Navigation. In that paper Montgomery related that he decided on the camber of a bird's wing, because it appeared to deflect the air downward so that it rode on the crest of an atmospheric wave, a concept now called dynamic soaring. Montgomery described how he set up his wing in a strong wind and released handfulls of eiderdown, from his mother's best pillow, studying the flow pattern. Next he rigged a heliostat device to reflect sunrays through a crude wind tunnel, while sifting dust particles into one end.

Amazed at this original research by a lone youth in California, Chanute offered to help him with his areonautical investigations, but Montgomery had already accepted a professorship at Santa Clara Jesuit College and abandoned further experimentation until 11 years later. In 1904 he designed and built a full-sized tandem wing aircraft, similar to the steam-powered model aerodromes of Professor Langley, and flew it over the San Juan Mountains, some 100 miles from Santa Clara, enlisting nearby ranchers for a ground crew. Said Montgomery: "In making these flights I simply took the aeroplane and made a running jump. The tests were discontinued when I put my foot in a squirrel hole and hurt my leg." Montgomery applied for a United States Patent on his tandem glider, the *Santa Clara;* it was granted on September 18, 1906. This machine was a thing of fragile beauty, delicate as a dragon fly, with wing-torque controls, rudder and elevator. To raise money, he hired a troupe of circus balloonists to pilot the glider, which was slung beneath a smoke-belching bag built by Ed Unger, a prominent West Coast balloonist. An April 29, 1905, a crowd estimated at 15,000 people jammed the Santa Clara fair grounds to watch balloonist Daniel Maloney, resplendent in bright silk tights, ride the glider into the sky. A devout Catholic, Montgomery had the balloon and glider blessed, then signaled the ground crew to cut the ropes. Up she soared to the cheers of the crowd, with 150-pound Maloney gaily waving from the seat of his

Balloonist Dan Maloney (far right) and Professor John J. Montgomery (next to him in bowler hat), pose with two unidentified friends in front of the Professor's tandem glider.

45-pound mount. At 4,000 feet he cut loose, and for the next 20 minutes, Maloney put on the greatest show above earth—diving, banking, and performing breathtaking corkscrew turns. After covering eight miles, he came lightly to rest on his feet at a predetermined spot, less than a mile from where he started. Said Octave Chanute: "The most daring feat ever attempted!" Old Dr. Bell cried: "All subsequent attempts in aviation must begin with the Montgomery machine!"

Montgomery launched an ambitious barnstorming tour up and down California, giving more than fifty exhibitions with half a dozen balloons, five gliders, and three riders. The performers tried to outdo each other with daring maneuvers. Tragedy struck on July 18, 1905, when, unknown to Maloney, a tail brace was broken on launch. Maloney waved to the crowd as he rode into the sky, becoming a mere speck against the haze, oblivious of the warning shouts from below. When he cut loose, a wing folded up and the machine plunged to earth. Maloney was the third glider pilot to die, after Lilienthal and Pilcher.

Bad luck overtook Montgomery again the following year, as he prepared to glide across Santa Clara Valley from a greased launch rail on the side of Mount Hamilton, near Lick Observatory, a favorite soaring slope today. The ground suddenly began to tremble and shake; his workshop swayed and collapsed. It was the great earthquake of April 18, 1906, that destroyed nearby San Francisco. Five years later Montgomery once more resumed gliding, and on October 31, 1911, made his final flight in a monoplane glider, the *Evergreen,* one that had performed well on half-a-hundred hops. Some 20 feet from the ground, his glider stalled, according to witnesses, and "reared up, slid sidewise, and struck on one wingtip. A gust of wind overturned it, throwing Montgomery onto his head." A stove bolt pierced his brain.

Most people in the early 1900's believed the Wright brothers had finally solved the mystery of bird flight, but others figured they'd missed the whole point. One such skeptic was Professor Harry La Verne Twining, professor of physics at Los Angeles Polytechnic High School, who persisted in pursuing that old will-o'-the-wisp, the flapping-wing ornithopter.

Professor Harry La Verne Twining, a Los Angeles school teacher, built a wing-flapper glider in the early 1900's, but he never got it off the ground.

"The bird is a living machine," he once said, "immersed in an atmosphere of mobile and perfectly elastic matter, from which it obtains support by the expenditure of energy on the part of itself, whether flying or soaring." He pointed out that the resultant of all forces acting upon a bird's wing, whether flapping upward or downward, is "forward in the plane of the wing, along a line of least resistance."

Early in 1907 Twining was detracted from his study of wing-flappers by a more subtle mystery of nature—the weight of a mouse's soul. In the school laboratory, after his students had gone home, he busied himself killing mice, carefully weighing them before and after execution. He was startled to find that they weighed less after death. Excitedly he prowled alleys for stray cats, grasshoppers, any living thing on which to try his ghoulish experiments. They, too, seemed to weigh less after being chloro-formed. He called in reporters and revealed his great find—scientific proof of the existence of a soul! But later, he called them back, admitting an error —the weight loss was due to giving up of body moisture, not ectoplasm.

Back to ornithopters, Professor Twining, who in 1909 became secretary

Old Bill Martin in his *Old Gray Mare,* so named because he used his plow horse to tow it at first.

of the Aero Club of California, built a 35-pound machine with a wingspread of 25 feet, took it into the Palos Verdes Hills and futilely flapped until his arms grew tired. The next year he built another ornithopter, for which a United States Patent was issued in August, 1912. Said the Los Angeles *Daily Times* on August 13:

"Professor Twining has almost completed a machine which he believes will fly. The frail craft is equipped with two great wings that suggest some monstrous bird of prehistoric time. The wings, carefully modeled after those of an eagle, measure 27 feet from tip to tip. The inventor does not intend to rise far from the ground at first, and is confident that when he does get into the air there will be no danger."

Once more he pumped and pumped on the wing levers, but like the soul of a mouse, the ornithopter would not soar away. The "Flip-Flop," as reporters called it, became a museum piece, and the Professor busied himself, in 1910, organizing America's first aviation meet at nearby Dominguez Field.

Equally determined to conquer the sky, though in a less spectacular way, was William H. Martin, a bearded country surveyor from Canton, Ohio, who created a *rara avis* that performed like a kite when towed behind his farm horse, Old Bill. Martin's machine featured a triangular wing; beneath a monoplane of 32-foot span were two V-shaped "balancing planes" of extreme dihedral. Whether it flew because of, or in spite of, the unique design, didn't matter. What mattered was that it flew. Martin's wife, Almina, held sufficient faith in her husband's contraption to ride it on January 16, 1909, as Old Bill galloped across the farm—no doubt hoping to escape the monstrous bird pursuing him. Martin took the glider to a gathering of Aeronautical Society birdmen at Morris Park Race Track, in New York City, and amazed the crowd by flying it around the track behind a six-cylinder Kissel. The tow rope finally broke and Martin crash-landed in a picket fence; he gathered up the pieces and faded from the limelight. Dubbed the *Old Gray Mare,* his odd glider was patented in 1909. A model ended up in the Smithsonian Institution.

Monument to fallen pioneers of gliding stands atop Mt. Wasserkuppe in Germany, where soaring was born.

# 3/THE BIRDMEN OF HESSE

IN THE GERMAN HEARTLAND OF HESSE, nestled between the Fulda River and the Iron Curtain, lie the historic and beautifully forested Rhon Mountains, a volcanic upthrusting where slope winds flow steadily over the highest peak, the 3,117-foot Wasserkuppe. Here, in the early 1920's, originated the modern art of slope soaring, when the right man and the right machine appeared at the right place at the right time.

Wolfgang B. Klemperer was born in Dresden in 1893, flew with the German Air Force in World War I, and in 1920, back in civilian life, graduated from Dresden's Institute of Technology to become an assistant to the distinguished aeronautical engineer Professor Theodore von Karman, with whom he worked on wind tunnel designs of light planes and soaring craft. Forbidden by the International Allied Commission of Control to build high-powered airplanes, von Karman's group sought to keep Germany's highly-developed aeronautical technology alive, an enforced specialization that would lead to unique advances in sailplane design.

Klemperer was well aware of the rich potential of the Wasserkuppe as a site for slope soaring; as early as 1910, two Darmstadt high school boys, Hans Gutermuth and Berthold Fischer, had discovered that long glides could be made there with homebuilt machines of the Lilienthal type. In October, 1912, Gutermuth stretched a glide to more than 2,700 feet.

Gliding in prewar Europe was not confined to Germany; in 1904 considerable experimental gliding had taken place on the sand dunes of Breck, France, on the English Channel. There, Gabriel Voisin made successful short flights in a machine of the Wright type; the next year he flew a pontoon glider, towed behind a motor launch, from the Seine River. What little work was done was forgotten during the World War years, with the possible exception of that of Frederic Harth, a German youth who glided into a slope wind near his home at Hildenstein for 3½ minutes in 1914. Harth would later pioneer slope soaring, but it was Wolfgang Klemperer who really got things going in 1920.

In that year Oskar Ursinius, editor of the German flying magazine *Flug-sport,* organized the first glider meet at the Wasserkuppe, urging German youths to bring their bedrolls and machines for a two-month campout. Twenty-four turned up, some ex-military pilots and many with no flight experience. Two, who would become leaders in the new youth movement, were Peter Riedel and Wolf Hirth.

The first Wasserkuppe encampment took three weeks to get rolling, and by mid-August the neophytes were trying to outdo each other with running leaps into the wind and long slides down the sky. Prizes totaling 25,000 marks were posted by Ursinius for the longest flights, the greatest number of flights, and the lowest sinking rate. But the contest was far from encouraging. Scores of machines performed poorly, and one contestant, Eugene Von Loessl, was killed when his glider broke up in severe turbulence. Enthusiasm was dampened by the tragic accident and the meet would have ended then and there had not Klemperer showed up with his mystery glider, the *Black Devil*. The other contestants gathered around, staring excitedly at the odd machine.

Built by students who called themselves the Aachen Aeronautical Society, under the technical supervision of Professor von Karman, of the Aix-la-

Bungee cord launch crew watches German primary glider set off on flight.

Chapelle (Aachen) Technical High School, the Aachen glider was a thick-wing monoplane similar in shape to the JL6, a powered aircraft designed by Hugo Junkers. Its wings and body were highly streamlined to cut down parasitic drag; the wings, forward part of the fuselage and landing gear were constructed of plywood as a single unit, to give the craft strength to withstand a hard landing.

Klemperer proudly showed how the low cantilever wing was built on three spars, and how the wingtips were slightly reversed in camber for stability. Non-balanced ailerons were fitted on an axis sloping gracefully forward and downward like a bird's wing, to reduce tip vortex loss. Inside the cockpit they studied the stick and rudder controls, and underneath, the two rubber-sprung skids enclosed in streamlined pants that formed the landing gear. The wing loading, Klemperer told them, was only .32 pounds per square foot of wing area.

On the morning of September 6, a steady wind came up with the sun, and with the help of the other contestants, Klemperer set the *Black Devil* into position, facing the wind. He had brought along a length of rubber shock cord, which the youths fastened to the glider and stretched taut like a slingshot. At Klemperer's command, others let go of the *Black Devil,* and it swiftly catapulted into the morning sky. In their excitement, the launch crew raced down the slope of the Wasserkuppe as the strange looking machine floated lazily off, Klemperer shouting happily. The *Black Devil* sailed farther and farther down the slope, finally touching earth more than a mile away. The distance was measured—6,006 feet, a new world's record! Next day Klemperer flew again, this time staying aloft 2 minutes 22⅗ seconds, far short of Orville Wright's 9¾ minute flight in 1911, but still enough to renew the enthusiasm of the Wasserkuppe contestants.

The effect of the Aachen glider was immediate—construction got under way on similar types for the second Wasserkuppe meeting in 1921. In their zeal to design gliders with the lowest sinking speed, the Germans developed two basic types of machine. In one, the goal was to achieve a flatter glide ratio by reducing resistance to a minimum, through streamlining. In the other, they sought to reduce the wing loading and achieve a better L/D (lift to drag) ratio by making the wings longer and narrower.

Both types demonstrated their abilities in 1921, when 34 machines showed up at the Wasserkuppe. Of these, 11 passed the elimination trials, but interest focused on three distinctly different craft—Klemperer's *Blue Mouse,* a refinement of his *Black Devil;* an open primary type, the Munchen glider flown by Karl Koller; and another mystery ship call the *Vampyr*.

Surprisingly, the non-streamlined Munchen machine beat Klemperer's Aachen glider hands down in the distance contest with a flight of 2.5 miles in 5 minutes 5 seconds, and the two ended in a tie for the lowest sink rate, each averaging 80 feet per minute. Built by members of the Aero Club of Munich (Munchen), Koller's machine had the same wing area as Klemperer's but was 20 pounds lighter, and with five feet more wingspan had the higher aspect ratio.

More important to the history of gliding was the appearance of the *Vampyr,* designed and built by members of the Hanover Institute of Technology. The *Vampyr* was a well streamlined, high cantilever wing monoplane that resembled the wartime Fokker F3. Weight saving was achieved by landing on the fuselage, using footballs for shock absorbers. The pilot was almost completely enclosed by its small cockpit.

Determined to surpass the design pioneered by Klemperer, the Hanover group assigned its top people to the *Vampyr* project. Dr. Arthur Proell, chief of Germany's Department of Aeronautical Research, brought in Dr. Georg Madelung, an aeronautical engineer from the German Bureau of Aeronautics, who insisted that the *Vampyr* should first of all have a minimum sink rate. Working with Dr. Madelung was Walter Blume, a former *jadgstafel* commander who had served on the Western front, and two students of the Institute, Friedrich H. Hentzen and Arthur Martens.

The Hanover group could devote full time to the *Vampyr* project; German aircraft production was at a standstill under terms of the Treaty of Versailles, and all but 150 airplanes and nearly all engines and aircraft parts had been destroyed by the Interallied Commission. But to Blume this was the best thing that could have happened. "We could forget the inefficient relics of wartime," he explained. "The designer was free to make complete use of recent experience, to devise radical improvements."

Once more the wind tunnels at Goettingen came to life, not to produce warplanes, but to refine the design of a strange-looking craft that carried the wing on top and no landing gear underneath. The fuselage swept up sharply to support a high tail that carried no stabilizer, only a rudder and a balanced elevator. When all was ready, Martens drew the assignment to fly the *Vampyr* in competition with Klemperer's refined *Blue Mouse*.

On the first day Klemperer got the jump on Martens, with a record-breaking slope flight of 13½ minutes, the first to surpass the ten-year-old record flight of Orville Wright. But Martens came back with the *Vampyr* to beat

Klemperer with a 15-minute flight, during which he made two complete circles. Neither was a true soaring flight, hence no awards were given, but in the *Vampyr,* the Wasserkuppe pilots saw the shape of the future—the sleek Hanover glider had increased the 5:1 glide angle of the old Wright biplane to 16:1!

If the *Vampyr* proved to be a revolution in glider design, a brand new piloting technique also appeared a few days later when Frederic Harth, flying a machine he had built with the help of Willi Messerschmitt, soared for 21½ minutes along the ridges near Hildenstein, following the birds back and forth, circling, and finally landing less than 200 yards from his takeoff point. Harth had mastered the art of slope soaring; the era of simple downhill skysliding was over. Where Orville Wright had hovered in one spot for nearly ten minutes, Harth had learned how to exploit the winds that followed the earth's contours.

As in 1920, the 1921 Wasserkuppe meeting ended in tragedy, when a

Wolfgang Klemperer's famed *Blue Mouse* was the world's first streamlined sailplane.

tailless swept-wing glider flown by Wilhelm Leusch sailed out over the valley and seemed suddenly to be drawn into a seething cumulonimbus cloud. Caught in a fast-rising thermal, he attempted to turn away from the forces that gripped him, but too late. The wings folded up and Leusch plunged to his death. Those on the ground looked and wondered—here was something to avoid, danger in the wild sky. But a few had other thoughts: perhaps those same updrafts might be harnessed to soar to record altitudes.

Among those pondering how to harness the unpredictable gusts that blew over the Wasserkuppe was Wolfgang Klemperer, whose third glider, the Aachen *Ente,* carried a front canard surface, like the old Wright machine. Klemperer hoped that gusts striking this surface would tilt up the wing automatically to take advantage of the sudden turbulence.

On paper, Klemperer figured that because air forces are proportional to the square of the airspeed, he could achieve a net gain in height in gusting horizontal wind, but extended dynamic flight would remain the secret of birds like the albatross. Professor Walter Georgii, of Darmstadt, wrote in 1930: "The extensive efforts made from 1921 to 1923 to connect pulsating dynamical effects with the performance of man-carrying gliders did more harm that good to the development and reputation of soaring."

Once the true principles of successful soaring were recognized, amazing

The *Vampyr* in flight. Built by students of the Hanover Institute of Technology in 1921, and patterned after the Fokker F3, it was the first of the modern sailplanes.

results followed. In 1922, Hentzen and Martens, in the *Vampyr,* carried out the first soaring flights lasting over an hour. Hentzen's record flight of 3 hours 6 minutes, in which he attained an altitude of more than 1,000 feet above the hill, made the activities of the Wasserkuppe world famous.

The great promise of soaring flight in 1922 was short lived, for neither the knowledge nor skill necessary for true thermal soaring had yet been developed. Sailplanes remained tied to earth contours, rising as high as the slope winds would carry them, and no higher.

One man who turned his attention to the problem of thermaling was Professor Georgii, then director of the Rhon Rossitten Gesellschaft (RRG) Research Institute and head of the Department of Flight Meteorology at Darmstadt. From Darmstadt came such successful sailplanes as the *Konsul,* with a span of 56 feet and an aspect ratio of 18. The *Konsul* featured a long, elliptical cross section fuselage, a large rudder, and differential ailerons, and became the prototype for future designs of the Darmstadt school. The RRG later reorganized as the DFS, turning out a popular kit sailplane, the *Professor,* for home construction. At RRG was born the concept that a good sailplane not only needed a low sinking speed, but also a flat gliding angle, if long-distance flights were to be undertaken.

Rossitten, on the Baltic sea coast, became Germany's second most popular soaring site in the early 1920's. Here, on a stretch of windswept beach where shifting sand dunes often piled 30 feet high close to the surfline, gliders not only drifted along the dunes with the seagulls, but occasionally swept out over the heavy surf to enjoy a brief spell of dynamic soaring, following formations of pelicans, who seemed to travel for hours, barely above the waves, without a single wing flap.

A master at this technique was Ferdinand Schultz, whose crude homebuilt glider, the FS-3, was little more than a wing on an open wood framework. In it Schultz learned the nuances of dune soaring, and once stayed aloft 8 hours 42 minutes to win back the world duration record from the French pilot Alexis Maneyrol, who had slope soared 4 hours 21 minutes in a freakish tandem glider at Itford, England. Schultz later soared his machine 14 hours 7 minutes and once covered 36 miles by dune hopping, skimming over the wild sea grass atop the dunes. Schultz's technique was copied by Johannes Nehring, a veteran of the Wasserkuppe, who made extended flights utilizing dynamic forces of the wind blowing over the breakers, sometimes venturing 100 yards from shore.

With the rise of Hitler, German glider clubs were converted into the beginnings of the Luftwaffe. Note swastika on tail of primary glider, Zogling 38.

The glider meet at Itford in 1922 drew 35 entries, some of them on the lunatic fringe—one carried a large fan supposed to turn a propeller when the wind blew, in a kind of perpetual motion. Another was an ornithopter of 54-foot span. A record flight by Maneyrol provided excitement that continued after dark; he refused to come down until others on the ground yelled that he'd beaten the German record of 3 hours 6 minutes, set by Friedrich Hentzen in a *Vampyr*. In the air with Maneyrol was a British pilot, Squadron Leader Charles Gray, who flew a bastard ship built from the top wing of a Fokker D7 biplane and the fuselage of a Bristol Fighter. The Itford meet was hampered by an unprecedented wind shift. The normal, strong south winds decided to blow from the north instead.

A third national meet in 1922 was held in France at the Puy de Combegrasse, an extinct volcano whose conical sides did little more than split the wind rather than force it upward. Unlike innovative German sailplane designers, the French merely removed engines from light aircraft, and the results were far from satisfactory. However, one French pilot proved in Africa that an airplane could soar under proper conditions. On January 3, 1923, Lieutenant Alphonse Thoret, a flight instructor, cut the switch in a DH10 and stayed aloft 7 hours 3 minutes, soaring along the cliffs at Biskra, Algeria.

40

Interest in gliding spread to Russia in 1923 when nine machines appeared at the first U.S.S.R. meet at Usun-Syrt, near Feodosiya, in the Crimea. The next year 48 gliders showed up to compete in slope soaring from the summit of a 500-foot mountain. There Leonid Youngmeister stayed up 7 hours 31 minutes in a Moscovich glider of 44-foot wingspan, a copy of the German *Vampyr*. An unusual entry was a parabolic flying wing glider of 32-foot span, designed by Engineer Cheranovski, which soared one minute 20 seconds. Two pilots were killed in the 1924 meet. Slow starting and largely overshadowed by German achievements at the Wasserkuppe, Soviet soaring would eventually become a national sport in the 1930's.

Little technical progress was made in soaring during the years 1924 and 1925. Motorless flight sank into the doldrums as interest in both Europe and America shifted to light planes and flying family flivvers. Soaring might well have died altogether, had it not been for Professor Walter Georgii, director of the Rhon Rossitten Gesellschaft Research Institute at the Wasserkuppe. Professor Georgii sent glider instructors to the Crimea, to Vauville in France, and to a new American gliding school at Cape Cod, and further stimulated interest in soaring by giving technical advice to pilots in Hungary, Holland, and Belgium.

By 1926, the revival in soaring and gliding promoted a search for new ways to extend the utility of motorless aircraft. Throughout Germany, almost every high school had its own gliding club, a youth movement that would attain military overtones in the 1930's, as young men trained on gliders to become future Luftwaffe fighter and bomber pilots.

To fifteen-year-old Karl Brauer, the love of flying, not militarism, prompted him to design and build his own 60-pound primary glider in Germany in 1928. The G-1 *Albatros* was a contraption of primitive beauty and flew well, when Karl ran down a hillside carrying under his arms a craft that weighed as much as he did. Once in the air, he rode in a saddle and shifted his weight to maintain balance. Two years later he built a second glider, the SG-2 *Etta* (named for a sweetheart), complete with landing skids. In this machine Brauer barnstormed the countryside and met many of Germany's leading soaring pilots. Later, during the war years, Brauer led an exciting life—he helped design the world's first jet bomber, the Arado Ar-234; was captured by the Russians; escaped; became a postwar consulting engineer, and finally landed in America, back at work on motorless aircraft, this time kitelike military "paragliders."

Professor Georgii had long been curious about the dynamics of cumulus cloud formation. It was well known to power plane pilots that cumulonimbus storm clouds produced frightening updrafts in their seething interiors, sufficient to form giant hailstones, but the mechanics of what went on beneath these clouds remained a mystery. Clouds were visible evidence of air in motion, but Georgii could only guess how invisible thermal cells formed. Somewhere in the structure of convective air movement, he believed, lay a means of escaping from the restrictions of contour flying.

While the study of thermals was going on, other German pilots turned their attention to out-and-back cross-country contour flying, something that demanded the highest degree of pilot skill. First to accomplish such a feat was Johannes Nehring. In August, 1927, Nehring made a remarkable flight around the Heidelstein hill in Darmstadt, starting with a soaring flight down the south slope of the Wasserkuppe. Gaining an altitude of 450 feet above his starting point, he swung around parallel to the ridge, flying at right angles to the wind until he came to Munzkopf, where he rode a strong upslope wind to nearly 800 feet. From there he was able to glide to the Heidelstein and return to his starting point.

Two years later, another birdman of Wasserkuppe, Wolf Hirth, who had only one leg, executed a still more difficult cross-country flight on slope winds alone. Starting from the western face of Wasserkuppe in a *Lore,* he gained 1,200 feet altitude, then glided down to the Schweinsberg hill. On his return he lost altitude badly, and found himself 200 feet below his starting point. Twice he was forced to turn back over the valleys, seeking new slope winds, before reaching home base.

By flying from hill to hill, Nehring and Hirth showed that entire moun-

In 1928, at age of fifteen, Karl Brauer built and flew G-1 *Albatros* glider.

tain ranges could be traversed in motorless craft, but the technique required masterly flying. In the spring of 1929, an Austrian birdman, Robert Kronfeld, was first to cover 100 kilometers, a remarkable flight in which he used the power of slope winds blowing over ridges, knolls, hills, and dunes to carry him along.

It is curious that so little was understood of the structure of air currents, called thermals, at this time, for therein lay the perfect form of rising air in which sailplanes could reach the restless sky above, and there draw upon the bigger forces of the atmosphere. We know today that cells of warm air, called thermal bubbles, rise from the heated surface of the earth, and grow larger as they ascend, but in 1926, knowledge of thermal dynamics was limited to theoretical assumptions.

The first glider pilot to ride the awesome updrafts of a building thunderstorm was Max Kegel, remembered by Karl Brauer as a heroic fellow who used a pair of pliers to extract several teeth and who sewed nuts and bolts onto his shirt front for buttons. This man of iron was unnerved one August afternoon when a massive black thunderhead developed right above the Wasserkuppe, while he was out slope soaring. With a wrenching suddenness, Kegel felt his sailplane buffeted about and helplessly swept skyward, inside a powerful updraft. Moments later, he was engulfed by the boiling cloud, from which there seemed no escape. Finally, those on the ground saw Kegel's sailplane hurtle outside the storm cloud, a mere speck against the sky. He regained his composure and soared off across the Rhine Valley, landing a good 30 miles away.

Rather than encouraging storm-flying, Kegel's experience dissuaded others

A view of the Wasserkuppe encampment from inside a tent, about 1929–30.

from attempting to ride cold fronts that swept over the Wasserkuppe from time to time. Professor Georgii, impressed by Kegel's feat, nevertheless prevailed upon Nehring to determine the strength of the updrafts under storm clouds in a powered aircraft, gliding through thermals with the propeller stopped. On June 26, 1928, Nehring flew into the squall line of an advancing cold front, stopped the propeller and flew without loss of height for 15 minutes. By subtracting the known sinking rate of his aircraft in still air, it was determined that such thunderstorm lift was strong enough to sustain a sailplane.

Robert Kronfeld took a chance on the Professor's theory in August of that year, and made a flight from the west slope of the Wasserkuppe, as a large, building cumulus drifted eastward over the mountains. He circled beneath it, continually climbing, until reaching 1,400 feet above the starting point, when the cloud began to dissipate. He then glided off to the Himmeldankberg Mountain a few miles away, where he worked upslope winds until the next cloud came sailing along. He worked this new thermal to a height of 1,600 feet above the launch site, and from there easily glided home.

The real test was yet to come; both Nehring and Kronfeld had carefully explored convective currents and lived to tell about it—Nehring flying his powerplane through a line squall, and Kronfeld drawing upon thermal energy under cumulus clouds. Finally, seated in a new high performance sailplane, the *Wein,* Kronfeld calmly studied a line of building white cumulus, drifting like a row of castles in the air over the Wasserkuppe on the morning of July 30, 1929. Already, a competitor named Groenhoff had gone up with a passenger in his two-place *Rhonadler,* and climbed clear through a towering cumulus, emerging 3,750 feet above the mountaintop and landing more than 18 miles distant, a record for soaring with a passenger.

Soon Kronfeld was spiraling upward beneath a drifting cumulus, to more than 6,700 feet. He stayed with the cloud as long as he could, then broke off to ridge soar along the Threungerwald for another four hours, landing finally at Fichtelgebirge, some 93 miles distant. He had proved that soaring flight was possible across flat country as well as hilly country, by riding with an advancing front. Soaring had at last been freed from earth!

Kronfeld was exploring a new frontier, one in which unseen forces could tear the wings from a sailplane. On the next trip he wore a parachute, just in case, and while he did not need it, the chute afforded some peace of mind

44

as he flew directly in front of a fast-moving squall line. Professor Georgii had counseled him to stay well ahead of the clouds; extreme turbulence could exist inside them as the cold air tumbled across the hot countryside. Above the rustle of wind over his wings, Kronfeld listened to the advancing rumble of thunder, soaring in advance of the front as a gull follows ahead of a fast sailboat. At times, wisps of vapor reached out to overtake him. Rain pelted his face, and clogged the pitot tube of his airspeed indicator. He pulled away, and was amazed to find strong lift as much as two miles ahead of the front. As the day wore on and darkness engulfed the lonely birdman sweeping eastward across Germany ahead of the storm, he decided to come down. He landed near Hermsdorf, having covered more than 85 miles in 4½ hours of thrilling flight—a new distance record. He knew then, soaring had found its rightful place in the sky.

German soaring pilot Robert Kronfeld made the first 100-kilometer cross-country slope soaring flight in 1929.

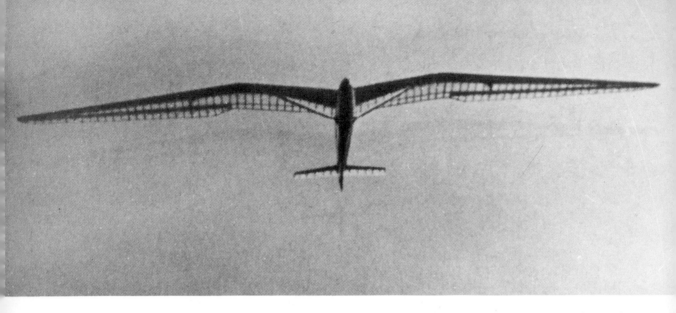

The *Minimoa* was among the first high-performance German sailplanes. It was designed for maneuvering inside small thermals, rather than for speed.

Kronfeld's search for the perfect sailplane led him, in 1930, to have one built with giant wings of 98-foot span. Called the *Austria,* it could virtually float on a zephyr, and was the largest single-place soaring craft ever constructed. The *Austria* attained a remarkable wing loading of only 2.82 pounds per square foot, but suffered from stiffness and controllability problems. On its last flight, Kronfeld soared beneath an immense thunderhead and was sucked up inside it. Fierce vertical currents sheared the wing in two places, forcing him to bail out.

Kronfeld went on with his pioneering work in motorless flight, and on June 20, 1931, entered his *Wein* sailplane in a British competition for the first double-crossing of the English Channel without power; the London *Daily Mail* had posted a cash prize of 1,000 pounds. Kronfeld simply had the *Wein* towed to 10,000 feet over the coast of France, cut loose and glided to England, then repeated the performance the other way.

In August, 1931, Kronfeld was back in the Rhon competitions, but not a storm cloud was to be found in the sky. Undaunted, he went aloft in the *Wein* and for the first time encountered the frightening phenomena of un-expected clear air turbulence—a thing that once prompted the great French poet-pilot Antoine de St. Exupery, to write: "Give me a good black storm in which the enemy is plainly visible. I can measure its extent and prepare myself for its attack. I can get my hands on my adversary. But when you are flying very high in clear weather, the shock of a *blue storm* is as disturbing as if something collapsed that had been holding up your ship in the air." Kronfeld was quick to utilize the dry thermals, as he felt his way through the sky, seeking out others that lifted him, only to glide off again to find a new invisible bubble of rising dry air. By this method, he soared 103 miles to Westfalen.

Wolf Hirth repeated Kronfeld's dry thermaling achievement, adding something he had developed himself—the trick of "centering" inside small thermals to extract maximum lift without venturing into dead air. He later wrote: "After about 40 minutes I found a thermal bubble which, without containing very much lift, was sufficiently expansive to enable me to remain within its limits. I had first exploited the idea of 'tight-circling' in America the previous year, and having further practiced this method in the course of five flights in Grunau, I was once again able to gain height steadily without clouds and independent of the slope wind. At a height of approximately 650 feet I left the slopes of the Wasserkuppe and circled steadily up to 2,000 feet. Five or six miles away from the Wasserkuppe it became apparent that there was no more lift in my original bubble, and I was unable to find any new upcurrents in my immediate vicinity. However, I suddenly caught sight of some butterflies that had obviously reached that height under thermal influences, and I hastened to make use of the same locality."

From that point, Hirth spent an enjoyable afternoon following the flight of circling hawks and other indicators of fresh thermals. By this method he covered 120 miles, finally landing in a small field near the Moselle.

Wolf Hirth's technique at tight-spiraling led to a new style of cross-country thermal soaring, in which speed is the predominant factor. Distance flights take time, and there is only so much sunshine in a single day to heat the ground to make thermals. Hirth recognized that speed in miles per hour was not as important as a fast rate of climb; by gaining altitude in one thermal more quickly, he had more time to hunt new thermals. Thus, he worked across country in a series of fast climbs and glides. In this manner, Hirth was able to cover 262 miles—from the Wasserkuppe to Zlabings in Czechoslovakia—in a graceful new craft, the *Minimoa,* which was especially designed for maneuverability in small thermals rather than for speed. He readily outdistanced faster sailplanes by his more efficient use of thermal power. Once Hirth had pointed the way to efficient cross-country thermal soaring, flights of more than 300 miles became commonplace—in one day

47

four sailplanes reached Brno, Czechoslovakia, 313 miles from Wasserkuppe, in 5½ hours, averaging 57 mph.

Something new had to be added to create a new challenge, and something was—goal flying. It was well and good to drift from cloud to cloud for hundreds of miles, but for a pilot to declare his goal, and get there by whatever route seemed best, required both careful planning and consummate skill. In 1935, Peter Reidel, a pioneer Wasserkuppe glider pilot, decided to run over to Hamburg from Berlin, a 164-mile flight. He made it. Erwin Kraft thought it would be nice to fly to Cologne from the Hornberg, 206 miles apart. On August 29 of that year he accomplished that feat, and set a world goal-flight record.

Russian achievements in long-distance soaring equaled and, in some categories, surpassed those of the birdmen of Hesse in the late 1930's, as European nations geared for war. Hitler's Germany was not alone in seeing a military potential in gliders for troop and cargo movement; the Soviets in 1935 developed a 180 place troop carrier and began experimenting with multiple tows of as many as 11 gliders at one time. An instructor at the Moscow Gliding School that year rode a storm front on a thrilling 106-mile night flight, following bonfires across the Moscow Basin, to begin a series of Soviet record distance flights that culminated on July 6, 1939, with a remarkable 465½-mile glide by Olga Klepikova, who maneuvered her *Rot-Front 7* sailplane from Moscow to Otradnoie, near Stalingrad—a women's distance record that still stood in 1970.

A variation on the theme of goal flying was introduced in 1936—a sailplane tour over a prescribed course, to be flown within a specified time with scheduled stops, disregarding weather and terrain. The first such tour, 432 miles in length, was completed by four pilots who thermal-hopped their way from Darmstadt back to Darmstadt, by way of Wurzburg, Munchen, Augsburg, Stuttgart, and Mannheim. The following year, half a dozen sailplanes, including a two-seater, made their way across the Alps. If the 1935 Rhon meet was notable for its number of distance flights—209 traveled more than 100 kilometers—19 pilots in 1937 declared their goal as Nurnberg, some 100 miles distant, and made it.

By 1938, sailplanes were being put to scientific use in a dramatic exploration of the inner workings of thunderstorms. More than 40 flights were

In 1939, Russian soaring champion Olga Klepikova flew her *Rot-Front* 7 sailplane
465½ miles from Moscow to Otradnoie, to set a women's distance record which still
stands today.

Nazi-sponsored gliding clubs used advanced trainers like this sailplane.

made above 13,000 feet, and one pilot, Captain Walter Drechsel, of the Luftwaffe, battled his way through turbulence to claim a new altitude record of 21,398 feet. Many thunderstorm penetration flights were "blind" instrument flights, a difficult technique in smooth stratus, to say nothing of controlling a sailplane in the buffeting turbulence of a cumulonimbus ice factory.

On one unforgettable afternoon, when a towering anvil-shaped cloud boiled and throbbed above the Wasserkuppe, a number of pilots donned their parachutes and launched into the wild sky to probe its interior. One by one they were sucked inside the seething vapors to vanish in a churning blackness, where energies greater than that of a hundred atomic bombs were being unleashed. Stabbing lightning glowed eerily about the sailplanes and the heavens thundered. Violent updrafts hurtled them higher and higher, through stinging raindrops and pelting hailstones. The pilots suffered from lack of oxygen; their controls stiffened with ice. Most of them managed to escape the raging thunderhead, but in his anger, Zeus, the thundergod, exacted a terrible toll for this invasion of his domain—snapping the wings from three sailplanes. The birdmen, Lemm, Schultz, and Bleh, kicked free of the wrecked gliders and plunged into the darkness, tugging on their parachute ripcords. For nearly an hour they rose and fell helplessly, inside the electrically-charged arena of death, then one by one dropped to earth. Their bodies were found later; one was charred by lightning, the others had frozen to death.

These men did not die in a reckless search for thrills. Said Professor Georgii: "Such experiences will give a new generation of flying men a body of weather wisdom by which they may safely meet and even turn to useful purpose the atmospheric disturbances so frequently met in air transport today . . . The true meaning of 'air sense' lies in this conquest of the variable atmosphere by the soaring pilot. Just as the master of a great liner must serve an apprenticeship in sailing ships to learn the secret of sea and wind, so should the air transport pilot practice soaring flights to gain wider knowledge of the air currents, to avoid their dangers, and adapt them to his service."

Atop the Wasserkuppe today, stands a rocky cairn topped with a bronze condor intently facing the winds from the west. The monument is a tribute to the heroic birdmen of Hesse, who gave their lives probing the unknown frontiers of the sky.

The Schweizer 1-34 is a new single-place sailplane designed to meet International Standard Class requirements, and is widely used in all types of soaring.

# 4/THE AMERICAN WAY

IN THE UNITED STATES, as in Germany, gliding was looked upon, in the years before World War I, as little more than a sport for youngsters, like tobogganing or sledding. Orville Wright's hovering flight of nearly ten minutes in 1911, produced a flurry of magazine articles offering plans for homebuilt hang gliders and primary trainers that spread the gospel across the land, but not until news of successes at Wasserkuppe reached America did things get rolling.

In September, 1922, Glenn Curtiss flew his Hydro-Sailplane over Manhasset Bay, near Port Washington, New York, towed behind a motorboat at 20 miles an hour. But he achieved little more than Gabriel Voisin had in France, nearly two decades before, making short glides of less than ten seconds after release from the tow rope 20 feet above the water. On the West Coast, an early birdman named Phil Parmalee made a number of successful glides in a Wright machine in 1910, during the world's first international aviation meet at Dominguez Field, near Los Angeles. Interest in gliding continued there sporadically until, in 1923, the National Aeronautic Association and United States Weather Bureau, canvassing the country for a good slope soaring site, found a hill near Oakland that met its requirements. The soaring committee, headed by Orville Wright, wanted a field on a long ridge with a 1,000-foot drop into the prevailing wind, near sea level. On July 10–15 a number of primary gliders met there to compete for $5,000 in prizes offered by the city of Oakland.

While thousands of German youths were learning to glide in the late 1920's, the scene in America was far different. Organized gliding clubs simply did not exist; public and government apathy prevailed; an estimated 2,000,000 air-minded American youths were spending $75,000,000 a year building and flying model airplanes.

The author joined such a model airplane club at Fairfax High School in

Los Angeles, California, in 1928, and was inspired by a *Popular Mechanics* article to build the wing of a primary glider in the school woodshop, with a buddy, Clarence Branesky. Our family moved east before the glider was finished, but members of a model plane club at nearby Loyola University completed the machine, which flew well.

At that time, considerable soaring activity took place on an open hill sloping gently into westerly winds that blew across the nearby Palos Verdes Peninsula. A flurry of interest in gliding also stemmed from the transatlantic solo flight of Charles Lindbergh in 1927; Lindbergh himself often soared at Palos Verdes with his wife, Anne.

Lindbergh was introduced to soaring by Hawley Bowlus, plant manager for the Ryan Aircraft Company in San Diego, who had directed construction of Lindbergh's famous ocean-spanning *Spirit of St. Louis*. Bowlus, a World War I military pilot, probably did as much for soaring in America as anyone. His gliding experience dated back to 1910, when air-minded Los Angeles sponsored an annual high school kite-flying contest. Hawley

This primary type glider is being rigged for takeoff at Palos Verde Hills, near Los Angeles, 1930.

Anne Lindbergh in Bowlus sailplane in which she won the first American glider license for women. At rear are Hawley Bowlus (left) and Charles Lindbergh (right).

won the first meet, riding a Curtiss-type biplane glider at the end of a rope held by his brother, Glenn.

Bowlus designed and built the first of a series of beautifully streamlined sailplanes in 1928. Called the *Falcon,* it was a high-wing craft with move-able wingtips for ailerons. In this ship Lindbergh soared 31 minutes along the cliffs at Point Loma. He climbed 150 feet, remained above his point of departure more than five minutes, and landed back where he started, to earn the ninth first class glider pilot's license issued in the United States (Bowlus held License No. 2). Anne Lindbergh, on the same day became the first woman in the United States to win a glider license, remaining aloft nine minutes.

Bowlus' first high-performance sailplane was *Number 16* (he'd built 15 others before it) and was the sire of a series of successful soaring craft that did much to stimulate the sport throughout America in the 1930's. Most popular was the *Baby Albatross,* which enthusiasts could buy in kit form for $385; hundreds were built by amateurs prior to World War II, and many are flying today. The *Baby Albatross* featured a high-lift, low-drag Gottingen 535 airfoil, graceful 44-foot wings with elliptical tips, an enclosed cockpit, and a tail hung on a long boom. Its performance equaled that of the best European craft, with a sink rate of 2.7 feet per second and 20:1 glide angle.

Hawley Bowlus's *Baby Albatross* slope soaring along cliffs at Torrey Pines, California. Enthusiasts could buy it in kit form for $385.

Charles Lindbergh, Hawley Bowlus, and friends set up sailplane at Lebec, California.

Bowlus' next model was the *Senior Albatross,* a 60-foot span sailplane, three of which were built in a new plant in San Fernando Valley. One was purchased by Warren Eaton, first president of the Soaring Society of America; another was lost in the breakers at Palos Verdes; and the third was bought by Richard H. du Pont of Wilmington, Delaware, a leading eastern soaring pilot who flew the craft from Elmira, New York, to Fredericksburg, Maryland for a record distance of 106 miles. A *Senior Albatross* is on display today at the National Air and Space Museum in Washington, representative of America's growing prewar leadership in the sport of soaring.

Another popular California soaring site was at Arvin, in the lower San Joaquin Valley, where winds blew up the western slope of the Tehachapi Mountains. Bowlus and Lindbergh frequently flew there, and from a nearby hillside at Lebec. One day when a storm front moved in from the Pacific, Woody Brown, in a *Super Albatross,* and John Robinson, in a *Zanonia,* rode the lift of the advancing cold air mass from Arvin all the way to 29 Palms, 170 miles distant.

Today, some of the most popular western soaring sites are located east of the Tehachapis on the lower Mojave Desert, where slope winds, desert thermals, and mountain waves combine to offer a variety of currents for cross-country soaring. Another popular West Coast site during the depression years was Point Loma, where Bowlus checked out the Lindberghs. There, on April 29, 1930, Jack Barstow flew a Bowlus sailplane on a remarkable flight that ended at 4 A.M. the next day. He recalled later that "darkness came . . . rain in heavy gusts blew in from the sea, and the wind stiffened. I had been up more than four hours, and it seemed possible I could break the American record of 9 hours 5 minutes 32 seconds made by Hawley Bowlus. I could see the lights of the cars below me, and hear the roar of the surf; I was floating in a soft mass of gray down, listening to the whimper of the wind. I would climb until the lights below dimmed, then glide down and begin climbing again.

"Ten slow hours passed, with every nerve, every muscle working to take advantage of every gust, like being the mind and body of a bird. Several times I sailed out over the ocean, which I could hear pounding on the rocks below. I determined to stick it out and go for the world mark. I tried to fly blind, crouching in the cockpit so that my head and face were protected from the wind-blown mist, but found this would not work. About 3:45 A.M. the wind began to die down; I managed to stay up 11 minutes more, and finally landed near my point of takeoff, after 15 hours 12 minutes in the air, an unofficial world record."

The original Bowlus sailplane built in 1928. Wheels were used for auto-tow tests over the level ground.

On the East Coast, soaring got started in July, 1928, with the appearance of a German *Darmstadt* sailplane at Highland Light, Cape Cod. Its pilot, Peter Hesselbach, stayed aloft 48 minutes. The following year, when Professor Georgii's RRG group sent German instructors to the new American Motorless Aviation Corporation school, at South Wellfleet, Cape Cod, American students trained on German primary *(Zogling)* and secondary *(Prufling)* gliders launched with shock cords. In August, 1929, Ralph S. Barnaby soared 15 minutes 6 seconds to win the first "C" Certificate issued in the United States by the ruling Federation Aeronautique Internationale. Here too, Hesselbach soared the *Darmstadt* on a good flight of four hours, creating a wave of enthusiasm equalling the interest in California.

Dr. Wolfgang Klemperer, designer of the *Black Devil* and *Blue Mouse* of Wasserkuppe fame, pioneered slope soaring in the eastern United States during an exploratory expedition into the Allegheny Mountains in 1929, to demonstrate the latest German techniques in cross-country mountain flying. He flew an Akron *Condor,* built by an American firm, the Baker McMillen Company. Dr. Klemperer had come to America as an engineer for the Goodyear Zeppelin Company, and founded a soaring group at Akron.

Early American sailplanes were, in fact, not mere copies of German craft; at the University of Michigan, Professor R. E. Franklin developed a utility glider, introduced auto-tow launching for training flights, and did considerable research work with airplane tow techniques, first tried at the Wasserkuppe in 1926 by Gottlieb Espenlaub.

In the summer of 1929, the short-lived National Glider Association was formed, under sponsorship of Colonel Edward E. Evans of Detroit, and a search began for a suitable site to hold the first national soaring contest. Dr. Klemperer and Jack O'Meara tried one area after another, and finally found a region which closely duplicated the slope winds of the Wasserkuppe— Elmira, New York. There, on October 4, 1930, the German expert, Wolf Hirth, set off one cloudless evening when the wind was down, in his *Musterle* sailplane, and surprised everyone, including himself, by flying to Apalachin, New York. Here was a totally new technique—blue sky soaring —which required no search for slope winds, thunderstorms, or cold fronts. Uneven heating of the earth's surface created convection currents above plowed fields and other surfaces that absorb heat during the day and dissipate it in the evening.

O'Meara reasoned that there must be similar thermals rising above the concrete jungles of a big city, and to test the theory, he towed behind an airplane to 3,800 feet above New York City one cold February day, cut loose and glided south along Manhattan's East Side. He felt certain that the populous island, surrounded by cold water, should act as a thermal furnace and send a chimney of warm air aloft; yet search as he might, there was not an ounce of lift to be found from the thousands of auto exhausts, furnaces, and other heat sources below him. Ahead loomed the spire of the Chrysler Building; in alarm he swung over the East River, pushed along by a strong tailwind. Suddenly he encountered the breath of the city, slanting off to the east, not directly over it! O'Meara approached a cluster of chimneys and felt an upthrusting. He circled like a hawk, rising past 2,000 feet . . . 3,000 feet . . . 4,000 feet, on the pulsing energy of the giant heat factory that is New York City in wintertime. He had altitude to spare, and glided easily to a landing at Glenn Curtiss Airport on Long Island.

Interest in utility gliders literally soared in the spring of 1930, shortly before the first Elmira meet, when Frank Hawks, a famous speed pilot, flew a Franklin sailplane, the *Eaglet,* coast to coast in tow behind a Waco biplane. Hawks took off from San Diego on March 30 at the end of a 500-foot rope behind the tug plane, flown by J.D. "Duke" Jernigin, with the idea of landing frequently to awaken interest in gliders across the nation. Things progressed well until the seventh day.

Franklin *Eaglet* being towed coast to coast with Frank Hawks at controls.

The Schweizer School at Elmira, New York, trained 4,000 students in 80,000 flights in 30 years with only one minor injury. Here, Erwin Jones, Schweizer Soaring School manager, poses with six students, who all soloed before their sixteenth birthday.

"Between Syracuse and Buffalo," said Hawks, "I experienced the toughest tow-flying of the entire flight. Twice I began to fear that I might be forced to quit the ship and join the Caterpillar Club, via my parachute. The wind was so strong and gusty that, nose the *Eaglet* down as I might, at sharper and sharper angles, I could not make it descend until the wind abated."

At one time, Hawks reported, the strain of flying blind was too much for him, after Duke had telephoned that he was tired of dodging mountains in the rain and sleet and wanted to fly the Waco through the overcast.

"Let's get down out of this!" Hawks finally pleaded.

"You're crazy," Duke replied. "I've been under the weather for the past twenty minutes!"

Only then did Hawks realize he'd been flying in the high-tow position, inside the clouds, while his friend was down below in the clear.

A crowd of 15,000 waiting in the rain in New York saw Hawks cut loose at 4,500 feet and glide down to land, 16 minutes later, delivering a sack of week-old glider mail from California.

The first glider meet at Elmira, in 1930, attracted national attention and produced the first official U.S. Soaring Champion, Al Hastings. Gliding clubs began springing up all over the country, and numerous small factories turned out copies of the German *Zogling* primary gliders. Three U.S. firms

61

began building sailplanes—the Bowlus Sailplane Company, in California; the Frankfort Sailplane Company, in Joliet, Illinois; and the Schweizer Metal Aircraft Company, organized in 1935 at Peekskill, New York, by three high school boys, Paul, Ernest, and William Schweizer. They soon moved to Elmira Heights, changed the name to the Schweizer Aircraft Corporation and became the leading sailplane makers in the United States. The Schweizer Soaring School, in more than 30 years, would train some 4,000 students, with a remarkable safety record of only one minor injury in more than 80,000 flights. The Schweizer school and factory were established at Chemung County Airport, directly below world-famous Harris Hill, the scene of annual prewar U.S. national soaring meets in which contestants utilized prevailing westerly winds, blowing across long ridges and glacial valleys, extending from the northeast to the southwest in the Finger Lakes region of upstate New York.

The first Schweizer sailplane, the SGP 1–1, was built in 1929, with the help of a group of Peekskill High School friends who belonged to the same model club. The wooden, wire-braced craft was flight tested in June, 1930, launched by shock cord. Their second glider, the SGU 1–2, proved a disappointment, although it used the same wing airfoil section that Hawley Bowlus had found worked well on his early machines—the USA 35A. In 1933, the Schweizer brothers completed their third glider, the SGU 1–3, affectionately called the *Brick* although it flew admirably after being towed aloft behind an auto. Not until 1937 did they begin building all-metal sailplanes, and by the time World War II came along, they were turning out training gliders for the military. Most popular was the TG-3A, a craft that served in the glider pilot training program as the venerable JN4D *Jenny* had served in the power pilot program in World War I. After World War II, surplus TG-3A's became popular low-cost gliders for numerous soaring clubs.

In 1932, the National Glider Association was replaced by a new group, formed to sponsor the Third Annual Soaring Contest at Elmira, with Warren Eaton serving as president. Called the Soaring Society of America, it has sponsored all national contests since, as a representative of the National Aeronautic Association and the Federation Aeronautique Internationale. Eaton lost his life in a glider accident on a demonstration flight at Miami, Florida, in 1934, and was succeeded by Ralph S. Barnaby, who made headlines in 1930 when he launched a glider in a drop from the Navy's rigid airship USS *Los Angeles.* In 1937, Barnaby was succeeded by Richard C. du Pont.

If ever a man was destined to play a leading role in soaring flight in America it was Dick du Pont, a handsome, blond, brown-eyed young man from a prominent Wilmington, Delaware family who decided to make his way on his own in gliders. His brother, A. Felix du Pont, was a sportsman-flyer and former test pilot for the Fokker Aircraft Corporation, but Dick du Pont found a different kind of challenge in the beauty and thrill of silent flight.

Peter Riedel, the veteran Wasserkuppe glider pilot, was invited by du Pont to attend the eighth U.S. Nationals at Elmira, where the two experts battled it out for the American Soaring Championship in 1937. In his sleek *Minimoa,* du Pont had worked his way along the treacherous currents of the Finger Lakes region almost to the Canadian border, at one time gaining lift from chimney smoke in the suburbs of Syracuse when almost forced to land. Riedel, who had been flying as an airline pilot in Colombia, South America, had learned to make record time across the Andes by following the giant condors, and at the Elmira meet, flying his *Super Sperber* sailplane, won the most points with a desperate seven-hour flight that covered only 124 miles under poor weather conditions.

During the Depression years that followed the 1929 stock market collapse, it was Dick du Pont who carried the burden of survival for American soaring, making news with one amazing cross country flight after another. On June 25, 1934, he soared along a cloud street stretching southeast from Elmira and landed 158 miles distant, at Basking Ridge, New Jersey, for a new world record. In the 1937 Nationals, he twice narrowly escaped disaster, flying inside cumulus buildups and virtually brushing wingtips with Riedel and with Lewin B. Barringer, another popular devotee of the sport.

In 1938, Barringer flew a perfect record goal flight of 212 miles, from a winch launch at Wichita Falls, Texas, to Tulsa, Oklahoma, flying du Pont's *Minimoa* both on instruments inside the clouds, and skimming the ground hunting thermals over plowed fields.

Such record flights became commonplace in the late 1930's; in June, 1939, Woodbridge P. Brown increased Barringer's goal flight record from 212 to 263 miles, thermal-hopping from Wichita Falls, Texas, to Wichita, Kansas. The next year, John Robinson soared 290 miles from Elmira to

Competition at Harris Hill among pilots flying 1-26 "one design" class sailplanes.

Mineral, Virginia, down the Appalachian slopes. Other pilots reached for the high sky—Robert Stanley climbed to 17,264 feet for a new single-seater record on the Fourth of July, 1939, and Barringer set a new world mark for two-seaters in strong wave clouds over Sun Valley, Idaho, climbing to 21,000 feet above sea level, or 14,960 feet above his starting point.

In their constant search for lift, soaring pilots soon developed a unique method of detaching thermal bubbles that sometimes cling to the ground, like jarring a soap bubble loose from a clay pipe; diving steeply toward the earth, they whirled back up in dizzy spirals that generated enough air movement to start the bubble of warm air skyward. This was a favorite stunt of du Pont, who was also to dispel an old superstition, that circling vultures overhead are waiting for death below. The fact is, vultures simply enjoy sharing a free ride in the same thermal bubble!

Barringer, who made his first soaring flight at the Elmira Nationals in 1934, became the first to soar across the treacherous Delaware Water Gap, in a Bowlus-du Pont sailplane, during an exciting flight down the Blue Ridge Mountains from Mt. Mongola in the Catskills, to Piketown, Pennsylvania. He narrowly missed beating du Pont's world distance record of 158 miles, but the skill he displayed established Barringer as one of America's leading birdmen.

All went well at first, as he rode a fresh northwest slope wind that flowed over the Appalachian ridges like an inverted waterfall and carried him across the Kittatinny Mountain fire tower. He startled the fire warden by yelling down as he passed over, 100 feet above, then caught a strong thermal that lifted him to 5,000 feet. He needed every inch of sky in which to traverse a dozen miles of unbroken forest to the Delaware Water Gap. Forests notoriously do not produce thermals.

He later recalled: "Finally, with the end of the stretch almost in sight, I find myself down close to the treetops. My last bit of altitude carries me just twenty-five feet over the top of the first of a series of hills. A slope wind gives me a boost. The glider creaks and surges upward. The treetops drop away. I give a yell and wipe the dampness off the palms of my hands. I have a few minutes now to start worrying about the greatest obstacle of the flight, which lies just before me—the Delaware Water Gap—the great leak in the dam of air formed by the Blue Ridge range. For a stretch of four miles, I shall find no slope winds at all—and no place to make a landing.

The Schweizer 2-32 is a higher performance model than the 2-33; it has a 57-foot wing-span, and maximum L/D of 34 at 50 mph.

"I finally catch a good thermal and my climb-indicator needle jumps upward. I bank in a tight spiral to stay within the thermal. Presently I'm looking down at the Delaware Water Gap from 3,000 feet, and I turn the nose of my ship to the west. Ten minutes later I'm over the Gap—the first motorless heavier-than-air craft to cross this landmark. I've got the ridge again, and that northwest wind, so I soar along at 500 feet above the ridge."

Barringer's flight came to an end in mid-afternoon, 6 hours 45 minutes after launch, in a small field where a barking dog and a farmer greeted him with considerable astonishment. "You got engine trouble?" the farmer asked. Barringer finally convinced him that he'd come all the way down from New York State on wind power alone.

The growing number of distance, endurance, and altitude record flights made in America in those easy-going prewar years, were established primarily by an elite group of sportsmen-pilots. Whereas Germany's rebuilding Luftwaffe had created a pool of 186,000 glider pilots, as of July 22, 1940, the U.S. Civil Aeronautics Administration could list only 124 licensed gliders, and 120 private and 45 commercial glider pilots. With the world gearing for war, millions of American youths were still playing with model airplanes, and those who believed gliders had a place in national defense were laughed at.

The XCG-16, cargo glider utilized during World War II, carried a large payload within a limited space. Richard C. du Pont was killed in test flight when craft stalled and spun.

# 5/WINGS OF WAR

*You Too Can Soar To Victory On Silent Wings!*
*Be A Flying Commando!*
World War II recruitment poster.

ON AUGUST 1, 1929, F.W. Pawlowski, Director of the newly formed National Glider Association, sat down and wrote a letter to Major General J.E. Fechet, crusty Chief of the Air Corps in Washington, D.C., inviting Air Corps participation in the first Elmira soaring meet. Why not, Pawlowski pressed, train pilots on gliders as the Germans were doing? General Fechet's reply was curt: "It is not believed that any good purpose would be served by introducing the use of gliding in the Army flying schools."

If that were not enough to quiet the matter, a firm directive was issued by the Adjutant General on December 28, 1931: "Except on specific permission from the War Department, Army personnel are *prohibited* from participating in any form of glider flying in other than government-owned aircraft."

For the remainder of the 1930's the U.S. military mind remained closed to the subject of gliders; their tremendous potential as military weapons simply did not occur to men accustomed to the snarling bark of Curtiss Hawks. Then suddenly it was 1939, and the reality was Hitler's Panzer divisions, Stuka dive bombers, and secret "whistling death" gliders that could bring about the downfall of a modern fort in a single day. Poland collapsed, and Norway, and then the Benelux countries. The Nazi war machine crunched over the Netherlands and into Belgium. Finally in its path stood mighty Eban Emael, Belgium's impregnable underground fortress, whose big guns covered the bridges of the key Albert Canal. Early on May 10, 1940, before daylight, the distant drone of Luftwaffe aircraft throbbed across the night sky, and went away. Nervous guards resumed patrols, unaware of what lurked in the darkness overhead. Then, one by one, giant troop gliders whistled out of the night to land behind each strategic bridge; others sat down directly on top of Eban Emael, unseen and unheard by the garrison. Nazi troopers poured out of the gliders and tossed grenades into the muzzles of the big guns. Within minutes they had taken the fort intact.

Shocked awake, isolationist America finally began to consider a glider training program, to be sponsored by the National Youth Administration, while Congress studied bills to establish government-sponsored soaring societies, like those in prewar Germany.

Oddly enough, it was that unique Army ground vehicle, the four-wheel-drive *Jeep,* that got the Army Glider Program rolling. In February, 1941, Major General Henry H. (Hap) Arnold, Deputy Chief of Staff for Air, jotted a memo to Major General G.H. Brett, Acting Chief of Air Corps: "I would like very much to have a small, light *Jeep* constructed . . . *Jeep* to carry two men and have light armor and guns. This *Jeep* should be designed and constructed with a view of fitting wings to it so that we can take it off as a glider and drop it as a glider. Having dropped as a glider, it lands on a field somewhere, sheds its wings and goes around as a *Jeep.*"

General Brett bucked the memo along to the Materiel Division at Wright Field, Ohio, and thus was born what has been called "perhaps the most controversial training program every undertaken by the Army Air Forces." Bids went out to prospective glider manufacturers to design and build flying *Jeeps,* while the Army suddenly found itself embarrassed at not having a single rated glider pilot—because of the 1931 War Department restriction on glider flying by Army personnel. On June 5, 1941, the ban was quickly lifted and a dozen Air Corps officers were sent off to learn the secret of the birds, six at the Elmira Area Soaring Corporation school, at Harris Hill, and the other six at the Frankfort Sailplane Company school in Joliet.

A BT-13 basic trainer being towed as a glider.

Procuring military gliders and training pilots to fly them was an unprecedented challenge to the Air Corps; the only prior experience it had with them was back in 1922, when Glenn Curtiss modified his hydroplane glider into a tow target; thirteen of these were built at McCook Field.

By mid-May, 1941, eight two-place training gliders had been ordered from four companies, and bids went out to 11 aircraft firms for both eight and 15-place tactical "flying *Jeeps.*" Only four companies responded— Waco, Bowlus, Frankfort, and the St. Louis Aircraft Corporation; other firms were too busy with combat plane production.

Out of the initial confusion came a grandiose scheme to darken the skies with a thousand gliders, which meant finding 1,000 glider pilots to fly them, the goal in early 1942. One month later, that objective was tripled, and by May they were screaming for a staggering total of 6,000 glider pilots. The most notable aspect of the mighty effort was that it existed on paper only—there was no detailed plan for glider pilot training, beyond the dozen officers flying at Elmira and Joliet!

This was the picture when the author, early in 1942, bravely approached a recruiting center in downtown Los Angeles, and tried first to join the Navy's plush "Yacht Patrol" that somebody had told him about.

"Hey, Clarence!" the man at the desk yelled to an aide, when he'd stopped laughing. "Come here and listen to this guy! He wants to fight the war off Catalina lookin' for subs on Bing Crosby's yacht!"

I told the Navy what to do with their boats and took my talents elsewhere, namely, to the Army Air Forces, who shook their heads. "Sorry, at twenty-seven you're an old man. But wait a minute," the old Sarge added, fishing in a bottom drawer. "Here's somethin' just come down from Fort Logan, Utah." It was a beautiful pamphlet that promised:

"YOU TOO CAN SOAR TO VICTORY ON SILENT WINGS!"

Excitedly I read how in six weeks I'd be a Staff Sergeant and pretty soon a Warrant Officer with silver glider pilot wings. And so I enlisted.

Six months later, not six weeks later, I was still not a Staff Sergeant, in fact had not yet seen any silent wings. We learned to fly at a Civilian Pilot Training camp in Owens Valley, tasting the fantastic wave lift behind the mighty Sierra Nevada, in a puddle jumping Interstate S1A, fondly called the *Maytag Messerschmitt.* But the days and weeks and months dragged until we finally found ourselves in Stuttgart—Arkansas. It transpired that in their zeal, the Army Air Forces somehow over-recruited—10,294 student pilots were committed to glider training. More than half were herded into "pools" deep in the heart of Texas, Arkansas, and elsewhere.

In a secret report, *The Glider Pilot Training Program, 1941 to 1943,* compiled by the Army Air Forces, and since declassified, it is stated truthfully that training went so slowly that it took nine months to process a student—three months in actual training and six months in the pools. These were not swimming pools; they were tarpaper barracks, in remote regions of a land that time forgot, where a "serious morale problem" existed and "utter discouragement" was everywhere evident, because of the unfulfilled "glittering promises of training within six weeks and rapid advancement."

Morale? Permanent KP duty was *sought after;* lieutenants were punched in the nose in the hope of getting shipped overseas; AWOLS and suicides were an alarming reality. Continual shipping from base to base fouled up personnel records and pay was months behind. With money from home, a few of us rented Piper Cubs from "Doc" Dockery, who ran a small airport near Stuttgart, and buzzed freight trains in death-defying head-on chicken runs.

At Stuttgart we finally got to see a genuine glider—a flying boxcar affair called the CG-4A. But by then the craft was grounded as unairworthy, and besides, the AAF had decided at last that it had too many glider pilots on hand. In February, 1943, a Glider Survey Board of eight officers visited all 13 pools for friendly little chats with 7,058 frustrated trainees.

"We've decided to shut down the program," the smiling chicken colonels clucked. "You have your choice of transferring to flexible gunnery training, Officer Candidate School or, oh, any number of nice assignments. And, if any of you men are yellow enough to want a discharge, put your hand up!" By actual count, 1,147 hands shot up (including mine); these were patriotic volunteers from civilian life, not draftees, nor had they transferred to gliders from career Army jobs. It was my fate to end up with the Royal Air Force, as a flight instructor, and to resolve never again to volunteer for anything.

Turbulent as the glider training program was, it finally began to shape up under the leadership of Major Lewin B. Barringer, in civilian life a leading soaring pilot, who served as coordinator of the glider program until lost at sea in a flight over the Caribbean in January, 1943. Working closely with General Hap Arnold, Major Barringer found that a deep resentment existed

72

Aeronca TG-5 after its first test tow aloft. Maurice Fry, test pilot, is in the cockpit, while Major Lewin Barringer, head of the USAF Glider Corps, stands second from left.

against anything having to do with gliders, among the officers of the Materiel Command responsible for approval of engineering designs and procurement of motorless craft. Word went out in January, 1942, that "Barringer swings a pretty big stick merely by virtue of being General Arnold's man."

Another ex-soaring champion to become "General Arnold's man" was Richard C. du Pont, who served as head of the glider program until September 11, 1943, when he too lost his life in an air accident. Richard's brother, A. Felix du Pont, Jr., who was transferred from the Air Forces Ferry Command to take over Richard's job, explained where much of the discord between the glider corps and the Materiel Command originated: "As you probably know, Richard was given the title of Special Assistant to General Arnold and kept civilian status. This permitted him to sign letters, *By order of General Arnold.*' Consequently a friction had grown up between him and Colonel Fred R. Dent, Jr., the man in charge of the glider section of the Materiel Command, because all the test work came under him."

In a corner of Wright Field, lights burned late at night in the Aircraft Laboratory of the Experimental Engineering Section (EES) that was

The Schweizer TG-3 was one of the first wartime glider trainers.

Colonel Dent's domain. While one group of engineers figured how to put wings on a *Jeep* for General Arnold, another struggled with the XTG (Experimental Training Glider) Project. The first contracts went to the Frankfort Sailplane Company for three XTG-1's in May, 1941, and the next month the Schweizer brothers contracted to build three two-place trainers, the XTG-2's. A second Schweizer contract was let for XTG-3's, which in turn led to the popular TG-3A production model. In October, another firm, Laister-Kauffman, agreed to deliver four XTG-4's and won a quantity production order for a craft that performed excellently.

All this design work took time; with a war coming on, time was of the essence. In Washington, the Civil Aeronautics Administration had a brainstorm—manufacturers of light planes were already set up for mass production; why not take out their engines and add a third seat up front, to make a three-place glider? Charles Stanton, CAA Deputy Administrator, called in Harold D. Hoekstra from the engineering department; within three days Hoekstra laid the completed design rework for an Aeronca glider on the boss's desk. "We did things a little faster then," Hoekstra recalled, "though it took Pearl Harbor, and months more, for Stanton to get the Army going

74

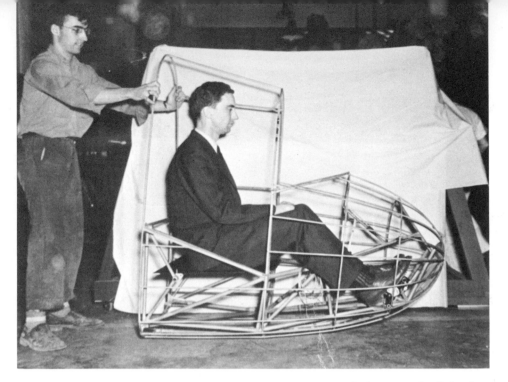

The above nose section replaced the engine of the Aeronca TG-5 to turn the light plane into a glider trainer.

on the idea!" Subsequently, the CAA engineering staff helped Piper and Taylorcraft redesign their standard light planes into training gliders; in all, some 700 aircraft were converted into Aeronca TG-5's, Taylorcraft TG-6's, and Piper TG-8's.

In May of 1942, a strange-looking, slab-sided, high-wing, flying boxcar, the Waco XCG-4 cargo and troop glider, arrived at Wright Field, months ahead of schedule. Colonel Dent was delighted to get anything that worked, and after a 220-mile tow flight to Chanute Field and back, with 15 passengers, he accepted the design. It would carry six men and a *Jeep,* which automatically swung the whole nose section up when driven out. On a crash-landing, however, the *Jeeps* were wont to break loose and hurtle forward, to the chagrin of, and often injury to, the flight crew.

Because of the urgency to get anything flying, production contracts went to 11 companies to build 640 CG-4A's even before the first flight test craft was delivered. And so began a rat race unequalled in the history of aircraft procurement, as first one design and then another was tried and eliminated in favor of the ugly duckling of the skies, the forest green, fabric covered, Waco *"Flying Jeep."*

The USAF finally settled on mass production of the CG-4A Waco troop carrier glider for combat use. The government spent $280,000,000 on 10,596 tactical gliders; $3,400,-000 on 1,086 training gliders in the Second World War.

The CG-4A, however, came in for extensive redesign to overcome its tendency to come apart on landings. A clipped-wing version, the XCG-15, was delivered in 1944 with improved ailerons, crash protection for crew and passengers, a higher tow speed, better payload, improved landing gear and visibility, and a pair of flaps for a better sink rate. But by then, the war was nearly over and the project dropped.

Shortly after the Pearl Harbor disaster in 1941, Colonel Dent flew to England to look at their big *Horsa* and *Hamilcar* troop carriers, and came home eager to build similar gliders in this country. Waco, in 1942, was given a production contract for a 30-place troop carrier, the XCG-13, more than twice the size of the *Flying Jeep*. Grossing 15,000 pounds, its 86-foot wings were made of plywood, its fuselage of welded tubing and fabric. Other firms went after contracts for 30-place gliders and failed miserably. One charged the government nearly a quarter of a million dollars for a carload of junk parts; another, organized with only $100 capital, charged Uncle Sam $426,230 for a glider whose wings broke off on its first flight test.

76

The XCG-10A was a remarkable 60-place plywood glider, designed for invasion of Japan prior to Hiroshima. Loading was from the rear and it could carry a 2½-ton M-22 tank. Below, a 155-mm howitzer is being loaded into the XCG-10A's rear.

In April, 1942, Jack Laister, a well-known prewar glider pilot, and his backer, John R. Kauffman, contracted to build three 30-place XCG-10 troop-cargo carriers of wood, with 105-foot spans. The firm found materials hard to get and by the time the XCG-10 was finished, Waco's big XCG-13 was already in production, and the project was dropped. The government looked kindly on Laister-Kauffman, however; they were doing a good job on TG-4A trainers, and besides, Laister had plans for an ever more massive 60-place cargo carrier, the XCG-10A, that could be loaded through the rear, with a 155-mm howitzer or a 2½-ton M-22 tank. Even the intractable Colonel Dent approved the design, and Laister walked off with a walloping $100,000,000 contract and a letter of intent to produce 1,000, to be used in a planned invasion of Japan.

For Laister, the order was vindication of his own design skill. In 1929, while in high school at Wyandotte, Michigan, Jack had worked on a primary glider, and two years later designed and built a utility glider with an enclosed fuselage. He worked his way through the Lawrence Institute of Technology in Detroit giving flying lessons, and there designed and built the famous *Yankee Doodle,* selected in 1939 by the Paris Aero Club to represent the United States in a glider meet. Success of the *Yankee Doodle* led directly to his war contract to build TG-4A trainers. A total of five giant CG-10A's had been delivered to the AAF at the time of the Hiroshima bomb, which rendered the projected glider invasion fleet useless. At war's end, Laister returned to his sailplane design work, with a popular kit soaring craft, the LP-49 *Forty Niner.*

The CG-4A *Flying Jeep* spurred a frenetic production race against time; Waco alone could not turn out the great number of troop-cargo gliders needed. With the big plane manufacturers geared to fighter and bomber production, a wild scramble began to find cabinet makers, furniture craftsmen—in fact, anybody with the slightest knowledge of necessary production techniques.

One company in Elwood, Indiana, won a CG-4A contract with no prior production record. Organized by a group of local businessmen who saw fat war contract money within easy reach, they tried to build a machine on the top floor of an abandoned warehouse, amidst a forest of pillars. Unable to get it out, they knocked a hole in the wall to make room for the wings. A full year passed, the company reorganized, and finally the contract was

78

cancelled in exasperation—they had blown $1,741,808.88 in government funds and delivered nothing.

Fortunately for the war effort, productionwise Ford Motor Company got into the picture late, set up a CG-4A line at their Iron Mountain plant in Michigan and built 4,925 gliders, nearly one-fourth of all tactical gliders delivered during World War II.

The Waco glider was a remarkable machine for all its functional ugliness, and in the hands of a good pilot could actually soar. Historian Richard Miller recalls the time Chester Decker, the U.S. national soaring champion in 1936 and 1939, was piloting a CG-4A in tow for the military, transporting ten fully equipped airborne troops on a cross-country flight to Wright-Field, Ohio. At 7,000 feet the air was bumpy with thermals, the sky flecked with good cumulus. The troops were airsick, but Decker was enjoying himself, remembering the thrill of soaring in such weather before the war. Suddenly the glider struck a particularly rough bump in the road and the tow line parted, with 50 miles yet to go. Rather than make an emergency landing, Decker calmly hunted up the nearest likely thermal, climbed to the cloud base, glided off to the next thermal, and so worked his way on to his destination, much to the amazement of the passengers.

Tragedy struck the CG-4A program in 1943 when Major William B. Robertson, president of the Robertson Aircraft Company of St. Louis, was accused of gross mismanagement for completing only six gliders of a large production order. Things picked up, and when 63 had been delivered, company officials decided on a public flight demonstration to prove their integrity. Robertson was a true aviation pioneer, who, with his brother, Frank, had been a wartime pilot in 1918. In 1926, the Robertsons had pioneered the air mail route between Chicago and St. Louis; one of their pilots was Charles A. Lindbergh, who had yet to fly the Atlantic.

On August 1, 1943, the Robertson factory shut down to permit its employees to watch their latest CG-4A perform over Lambert–St. Louis Field. A crowd of 4,000 assembled; newspaper and radio reporters gathered to interview luminaries invited to ride in the new motorless craft. These were William Dee Becker, the Mayor of St. Louis; Thomas Dysart, President of the St. Louis Chamber of Commerce; Max Doyne, Director of Public Utilities; Charles Cunningham, Deputy Controller; Presiding Judge Henry Mueller of the County Court; Major Robertson, and his vice president, Harold A. Krueger; and the glider crew, Captain Milton Klugh, pilot;

In the fall of 1944, the USAF had insufficient cargo planes to haul supplies from India over The Hump into China, so Air Materiel Command devised a plan to convert the DC-3 (C-47) into a glider, by sealing engine mounts; the XCG-17 was the result.

Lieutenant Colonel Paul Hazelton, co-pilot, and Pfc. J.M. Davis.

The band played, people waved and the tow plane, a military C-47, moved down the runway, the CG-4A following at the end of a 150-foot nylon rope. The aerial train disappeared, then recrossed the field at 1,000 feet. The glider cut loose and pulled up in a graceful climing turn, when suddenly the left wing collapsed, and then the right wing broke off. The fuselage plummeted straight to the ground, crashing before the horrified onlookers. All aboard died.

Subsequent investigation by a panel of experts, including Jack Laister, blamed the crash on a faulty wing strut fitting, built by a St. Louis casket maker. All Robertson CG-4A's, including those at Stuttgart Field, were immediately grounded. Another 95 were grounded shortly thereafter, pending an investigation of use of unauthorized materials by a brewery-turned-glidermaker. Columnist Drew Pearson wrote a scathing newspaper column charging that the entire U.S. Glider Program had been "woefully neglected."

Still more trouble was to come, this time on the West Coast, where Hawley Bowlus, in February, 1942, designed an unusual flying wing type 40-place troop glider, the MC-1. Organized as Airborne Transport, Inc., of Los Angeles, the firm became, in turn, the Albert Criz Company, and finally the General Airborne Transport Company, with officers listed as Bowlus and his two brothers, Glenn and Fred, a promoter named Albert Criz, and an attorney, Isidore Lidenbaum. A Chicago firm, General American Transportation Corp., owned controlling interest in GAT.

In December of 1942, Criz showed up in Washington beating the drums for the new Bowlus MC-1 machine, then ran headlong into Colonel Dent, who flatly rejected the proposal as neither accurate nor reasonable. The drag estimates were "ridiculously low" and performance characteristics "highly optimistic," Dent snapped, and further, the firm had inadequate financing, no engineering personnel, no definite organization or experience. To negotiate a contract with GAT, he charged, would be to "invite trouble."

At a Washington meeting of top brass of the controversial glider program, Major A. Felix du Pont, then with the Air Transport Command, voiced his approval of the MC-1: "We would certainly like to test a wing-design cargo-trailer similar to the one which is engineered by Airborne Transport, which we understand can be towed at 140 mph and has a 10,000 pound payload capacity." Colonel R.G. Landis, Chief of Staff, I Troop Carrier Command, added his voice: "It is reported to have much better wing loading than the CG-4A."

Colonel Dent's group at AMC was not about to let the General Staff officers ram the MC-1 down their throats. On February 16, 1943, Major General O.P. Echols, Commanding Officer of the Materiel Command, announced "a special investigation of this entire matter." Three brigadier generals had inspected the GAT plant on the West Coast, said General Nichols, and found the factory to be "a small store building formerly used as a dry cleaning shop. The building was a one-story affair, approximately 30 feet wide and 100 feet long, just large enough for the small glider they have built to fit in sideways. The visible equipment consisted of a couple of carpenter's benches."

One investigator, Brigadier General B.W. Chidlaw, Assistant Chief of Staff for Engineering, Materiel Command, thundered: "We refuse to be stampeded into dishing out a juicy contract unless the glider is definitely worthwhile, which I seriously doubt!"

This cargo glider, the XCG-16, was to be used as a long-tow glider for the invasion of Japan, but the A-bomb put an end to any plans for this craft.

Such criticism appears to have been partly justified; the design concept was ahead of its time, and certainly the clumsy Waco CG-4A could not have been used for the long overwater invasion of Japan, as then planned. A. Felix du Pont told the author recently that his brother, Richard, "knew Hawley Bowlus quite well, and he had taken an aerodynamics course under him at the Curtiss-Wright School in California prior to the war. [The MC-1] could carry two *Jeeps* and had made some thirty flights, I believe."

The first full-size MC-1 was constructed in the summer of 1943, and on August 25, Richard du Pont, then special assistant for the glider program, took photos of it to General Arnold, explained the circumstances under which it had been built, and recommended it be procured as commercially approved "as in the case of the DC-3 transports." Dick du Pont saw a great future in the MC-1 for transcontinental glider trains, and one week after his meeting with General Arnold took the MC-1 photos to General Echols, suggesting that a contract be placed by the Materiel Command for 1,000 flying wing gliders, the contract to be administered by the Department of Commerce.

Eleven days later, Richard du Pont was killed at March Field, California, where he had been conducting his own tests on the MC-1 in flight behind a B-24, flown by a friend. He had hoped to fly it coast to coast, to show its performance on a long tow such as would be required to invade Japan. Essential to its performance was a proper trim; du Pont had carefully placed shot bags in the cargo bay for the final test flight. With him went his Deputy

Director of the Glider Program, Colonel Ernest Gabel, and a flight crew from General Airborne Transport. Recalls A. Felix du Pont:

"The night before the accident, Richard had been discussing the merits of flying above or below the slipstream. At 4,000 feet above March Field the glider descended below the slipstream, but due to its clean design, caught up on the rope. When the rope jerked the glider, the shot bags moved aft making a tail heavy condition and the nose went up. He was busy moving shot bags. The pilot and the rope made the nose go down. On the next rise, the pilot cut loose and the glider went into a stall and started to spin. The pilot ordered the ship abandoned, and as you know, Richard's chute didn't open, though a couple of others did and a full report was written up."

Although two other pilots, Howard L. Morrison and C.C. Chandler, were killed with du Pont, his death, like that of Lewin Barringer, evoked a keen sense of loss across the nation. In an unusual tribute, the New York *Herald Tribune* noted: "Almost every day, to be sure, we learn of the loss of bombers or fighter planes over one or another of the combat zones and think of them, with a sinking of the heart, in terms of men sacrificed. Why, then, should the tragedy that has overtaken this particular aviator in an experimental flight etch itself so deeply on the imagination?

"The answer seems to be that, besides distinguishing himself as a pilot and promoter of air transport, he long ago became our national champion of what he himself called *pure flight*—the soaring from cloud to cloud in a sailplane. Among Americans he was the man-bird par excellence, the exemplar of a sport whose poetry takes the breath. So, his wings broken, he has fallen, and something beautiful, expressed in his daring and in the choice of his enthusiasms, has perished."

Despite the tragedy, GAT's Albert Criz continued his promotion of the MC-1. He finally won unexpected support from Major General B.M. Giles, Chief of Air Staff, who warned General Arnold that a real need existed for MC-1's, and directed procurement of an invasion fleet of 1,000 Bowlus-Criz gliders.

Opposition from within the Materiel Command was immediate and vehement, and General Giles rescinded his order on November 9. Instead, he ordered three experimental models, designated XCG-16's. Criz promised to deliver them not later than February, 1944, but three months after the deadline none had been finished. By the following October, cost overruns

The Flying Wing XCG-16 carried eight troops inside its wing for quick deployment, but the USAF said that cramped quarters induced air sickness.

brought the XCG-16 contract price to a staggering $2,150,000. Flight testing took place at Oxnard Air Force Base in California, and in August, 1944, four glider pilots, Hawley and Fred Bowlus, Paul Tuntland, and Harry Perl, proved the strange ship's worth when they sucessfully flew from March Field to Clinton County Air Base in Ohio in 13 hours 4 minutes, not including two refueling stops for the B-17 towplane. The end of Richard du Pont's dream project came on November 2, 1944, when an Army Air Forces Evaluation Board flatly declared the XCG-16 "operationally and tactically unsuitable."

There were other unique wartime glider projects, such the XAG-2 assault glider, a low-wing cantilever monoplane built by Timm Aircraft Co. of Los Angeles as an eight-place wood ship with crew compartment armor plate, two .30 caliber waist guns, and a twin .50 caliber gun turret, apparently meant to duplicate the feat of Nazi glider men who landed atop Eban Emael. General B.W. Chidlaw of the Materiel Command snorted: "This whole project of assault gliders with turrets, generators, radios, and so on, is nothing but a damn fool idea!" The program was spiked. In another scheme, three CG-4A's were fitted with twin 175-hp engines to become experimental power gliders XPG-1, XPG-2, and XPG-3, but none went into production.

From the entire tactical glider procurement program, the one ship that proved to be the workhorse of tactical invasion fleets was the clumsy green giant, born of General Hap Arnold's idea for a flying *Jeep*—the CG-4A. A total of 3,615 went to Europe, and hundreds more to the Mediterranean, Far East, and China-Burma-India Theaters of Operation. In all, the government spent $279,973,091.87 for 10,596 tactical gliders, $3,406,490 for 1,086 trainers. The courageous role glider pilots played in global warfare is told in the following chapter.

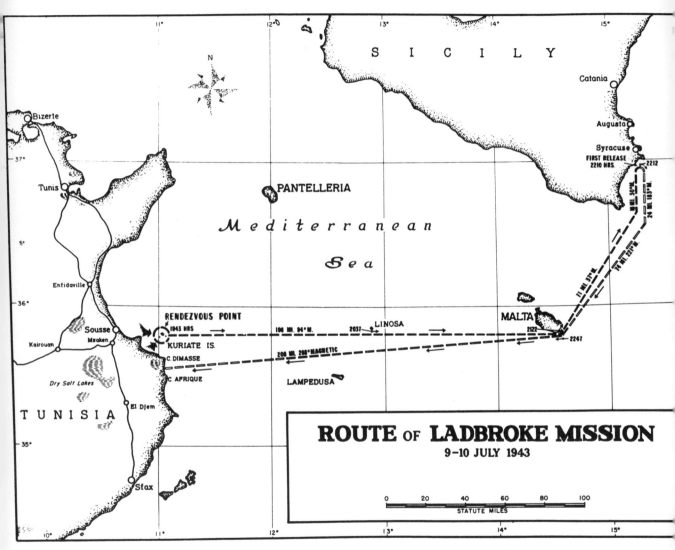

The Ladbroke Mission, the USAF's first tactical employment of gliders in warfare, was flown in support of a paratroop drop over Sicily. But the Allied Fleet opened fire on their own gliders by mistake, and the results were tragic.

# 6/THE MOONSET MACHINES

A LOW MEDITERRANEAN QUARTER-MOON hung in the humid western sky, peering down through scudding clouds partially obscuring the desolate, rocky Kuriate Islands, not far offshore from the east coast of Tunisia. Overhead droned formations of camouflaged C-47's, towing elephantine Waco gliders headed for their first combat mission. A few British Horsas orbited overhead behind four-engine Halifaxes, jockeying for rendezvous position in the glider train, to begin their long overwater night flight from Africa to Malta, and thence to Sicily. Their goal was Ponte Grande, a small bridge near the ancient city of Syracuse, where Allied paratroopers of Operation Husky would rain down on beachheads and drop zones to the south. The date was July 9, 1943; the time 10:43 P.M.

Sicily was selected at the Casablanca Conference of President Franklin D. Roosevelt, Prime Minister Winston Churchill, and the Combined Chiefs of Staff, as a logical Allied objective—an attack on the underbelly of Fortress Europe—following the bitter North African campaign. From the start, Operation Husky had been troublesome. A key part of it, the glider strike, Operation Ladbroke, was doomed to end tragically.

Flying low across the Mediterranean Sea, the Ladbroke glider pilots apprehensively studied breaking whitecaps, lashed by a 40-knot wind from the northwest. Salt spray whipped up by the propellers of the C-47's, skimming virtually on the deck, hammered back against the plexiglass windows of the Wacos, further reducing visibility. If all went well, they'd pass another small island checkpoint, Linosa, raise the signal lights of the Allied High Command base at Malta, then pass around the southern tip of Sicily to their release point, offshore of Maddalena Peninsula, across the bay from Syracuse. Four landing zones lay beyond; all were within easy gliding range.

Blackness settled over the glider train as Malta faded into the distance.

Once secured, the island of Sicily became the jumping off place for further glider invasions of Italy and France. Here a train departs Comiso Airfield, Sicily, 1943.

Crowded inside 137 motorless combat craft were more than 1,200 fighting men of Major General G.C. Hopkinson's British Airlanding Brigade, silently fingering their weapons, wondering what lay ahead. Hopefully, the mission would come off as well as the incredible Nazi sneak attack on Crete, when a mere 75 German gliders on June 20, 1941, captured that strategic Greek island as handily as they'd silenced Fortress Eban Emael. It was the Crete attack that established the glider as a revolutionary combat machine. Now American-built Wacos, flown by a mixed force of American and British pilots, were about to show what they could do. While the Nazi strike at Crete was an example of split-second timing, Ladbroke was destined from its inception to suffer unbelievable confusion, astounding errors of judgement.

British General Bernard L. Montgomery, to begin with, originally set up the Sicily invasion as an all-paratroop operation, and so picked the night of July 9/10, when a quarter-moon would set at half past midnight and cover their ground operations. Later, when Montgomery decided to use gliders, the British Airborne Forces advisor, Group Captain T.B. Cooper, RAF, protested in vain that a glider assault on a dark night with inexperienced crews would be murderous, yet the decision stood.

Secondly, Montgomery's last-minute switch from a paradrop to a glider mission reversed the roles of the 51st and 52nd Troop Carrier Wings; the 52nd, well trained in glider towing in the United States with the 82nd Airborne Division, was assigned to drop paratroopers in Operation Husky; the 51st, a veteran North African outfit with almost no glider experience, drew the Ladbroke glider run.

Thirdly, there was the dire warning from the Allied Fleet that any formation flying over their convoys lower than 6,000 feet would be fired upon as hostile aircraft. However, because at such height the huge formations would show up on enemy radars "like a herd of elephants on a hilltop," deck-level routes were finally authorized, chosen carefully to avoid Allied convoys. The route involved three sharp turns over water in dim moonlight, prompting Major General Matthew B. Ridgeway, 82nd Division Commander, to write later that "no American outfit in the whole course of the war could have flown that route sucessfully!"

Barely three weeks before D-Day in Sicily, the 51st Wing had begun intensive glider-towing training in Africa; the British glider pilots were totally ignorant of American gliders. A total of 500 new Wacos had been delivered from the United States for the Sicily invasion, but arrived unassembled, in crates scattered at North African ports hundreds of miles apart. Windstorms wrecked many gliders as fast as they were assembled; plane-to-glider intercom sets and essential flight instruments could not be found. Thus, when D-Day arrived, the British pilots were still poorly trained in Wacos, with barely an hour's night flying experience and no overwater release practice.

If Ladbroke got off to a precarious start, the Husky paradrops which Ladbroke was to support were having their own problems. The first drop, Husky 1, spread paratroopers over half of Sicily; one transport strayed clear to the toe of Italy. Husky 2 fared worse, due to a breakdown in communications. Admiral Henry K. Hewitt of the amphibious Western Task Force heatedly denied receiving any information on the troop carrier routes

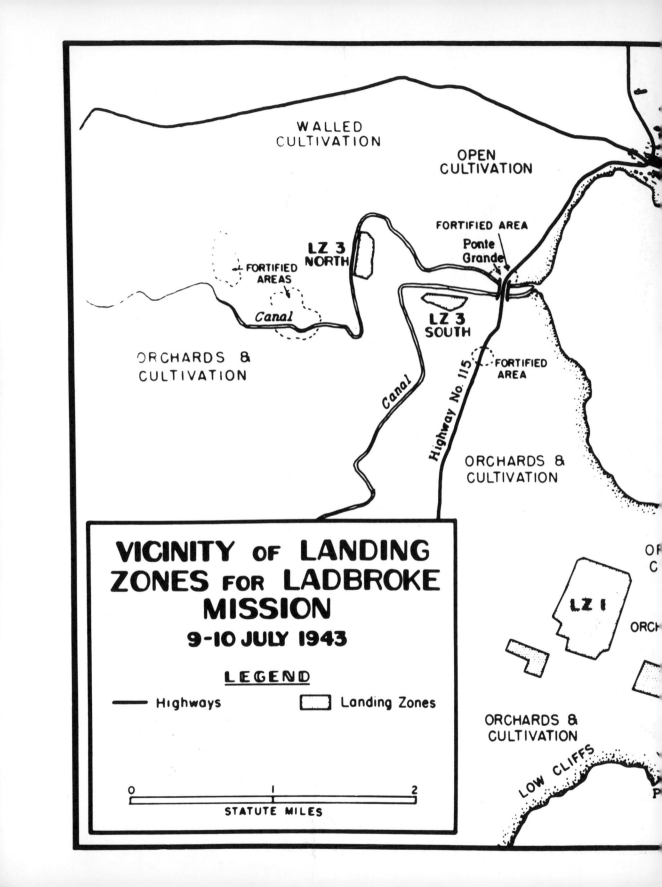

WALLED CULTIVATION

OPEN CULTIVATION

FORTIFIED AREA

Ponte Grande

LZ 3 NORTH

FORTIFIED AREAS

Canal

LZ 3 SOUTH

FORTIFIED AREA

ORCHARDS & CULTIVATION

Canal

Highway No. 115

ORCHARDS & CULTIVATION

OR C

LZ I

ORCH

ORCHARDS & CULTIVATION

LOW CLIFFS

P

# VICINITY OF LANDING ZONES FOR LADBROKE MISSION
## 9-10 JULY 1943

### LEGEND

——— Highways        ▭ Landing Zones

0        1        2
STATUTE MILES

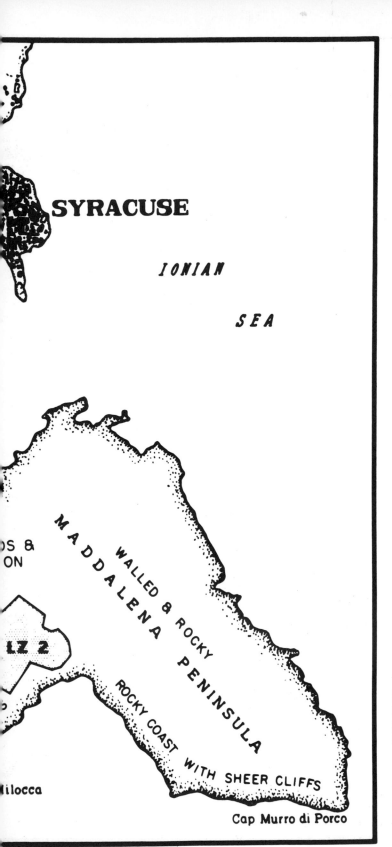

SYRACUSE

IONIAN

SEA

DS &
ON

MADDALENA
WALLED & ROCKY
PENINSULA

LZ 2

ROCKY COAST WITH SHEER CLIFFS

lilocca

Cap Murro di Porco

This chart shows the four target landing zones (LZ's) of the Ladbroke Mission, near Syracuse, Sicily. Few gliders reached their objectives.

until his fleet was at sea under radio silence. At first the Husky 2 pilots believed the mission could be a "milk run;" on their way to Sicily they joked and sang and practiced formation flying. As they approached the Sicilian coastline, a nervous ground gunner opened fire. Almost instantly, machine guns and antiaircraft batteries opened up along the entire length of the invasion beaches. The rear glider squadrons, still some ten miles offshore, became targets of wild Allied naval gunfire. Desperately, the C-47 tow pilots broke formation and took evasive action. Those who escaped ground fire along the beaches still had to run the gauntlet of navy guns. By the time Husky 2 had ended, an appalling loss ratio of 16 percent was chalked up against the navy, which won the reputation of shooting from the hip, without distinguishing friend from foe. One returning Husky 2 pilot remarked bitterly that "the safest place over Sicily was over enemy territory."

The first seven tow pilots of Ladbroke, approaching their target area undetected and undisturbed at moonset, considered themselves lucky. Then, awakened garrisons switched on sweeping searchlights, and antiaircraft batteries opened on the second wave of Wacos. Confusion reigned; the pilots were blinded by the lights and flares, and by their spray-coated windscreens. In the face of the dazzling pyrotechnic display, the C-47 pilots dropped their gliders and turned for home.

Operations planning had called for release of the Wacos at between 1,100 and 1,500 feet, but many tow pilots realized the northwest wind was far stronger than had been forecast, and so climbed 3,000 feet before cutting their gliders loose. Regardless, more than half the Wacos that reached the Sicily area that unforgettable night found themselves gliding through the darkness many miles at sea, unable to reach land.

General Hopkinson, leader of the British Airlanding Brigade, picked up by rescue vessels from the water-logged wreckage of his glider, cursed the 51st Wing pilots with every breath he could muster. The same men who had won his glowing praise the day before stood accused of running from enemy gunfire; the charge later resulted in brawls in many an English tavern, between Yankee troop carrier men and British Airborne.

The main blame for the Ladbroke fiasco fell on poor planning, in not allowing for a wind change and not dropping the gliders directly over the beaches, instead of more than a mile at sea. But the worst had happened— a total of 69 Wacos had to ditch in the Mediterranean; more than 300 troops were drowned. Another 49 Wacos and five Horsas reached Sicilian soil, with varied success; seven Wacos smashed into trees, two Horsas crashed into stone walls, and one Horsa flew headlong into a canal. The toll of Ladbroke was 605 officers and men, with 326 missing and presumed drowned. For that sacrifice, only five percent of the airborne troops reached their objective. Heroically, troops from one Horsa which landed precisely on Landing Zone 3, set up their big gun and captured Ponte Grande, Ladbroke's main objective.

Ladbroke was followed on July 13 by a second glider strike at Sicily— Operation Fustian—in which eight Wacos and 11 Horsas carrying guns, vehicles, and artillerymen joined an assault against the Primasole Bridge, over the Simeto River near Catania. Once more angered glider pilots ran the gauntlet of navy guns; this time more than 30 gliders were fired on. Despite the tragedy of the Sicilian glider operations, the lessons learned set the stage for the 1944 invasion of Fortress Europe, at Normandy.

Glider pilot in Waco CG-4A parachutes landing gear (actually, takeoff gear) over field; landings are made on skids that bring craft to faster stop in short fields.

Indirectly, Sicily produced one of the war's strangest glider episodes, involving a young Austrian commando, Otto Skorzeny, who had gained Hitler's favor as a Captain in the *Friedenthal* Special Formation Waffen SS forces. Ladbroke was a stepping stone to the invasion of Italy, where two weeks later, Premier Benito Mussolini was repudiated by Count Dino Grandi's Fascist Grand Council. King Victor Emmanuel III accepted Il Duce's resignation, appointing Marshal Pietro Badoglio as his successor.

With Mussolini hidden away in protective custody, anticipating delivery of Badoglio's government to the Allies, an armistice was suddenly signed on September 3. Hitler, fuming against Italy's "treachery," had a brainstorm; if Mussolini could be captured before the Allies got to him, he could become the figurehead of a new "Republican Fascist Party" to continue the war in Italy. To Hitler, the square-jawed Il Duce was the incarnation of Rome's ancient grandeur.

On September 12, while the Allies were pressing across the bloody 25-mile invasion beaches from Salerno to Agropoli, a strange drama was taking place in the Alpine resort of Gran Sasso. Skorzeny had found Mussolini's hiding place—a resort high in the mountain fastness. There, under heavy guard, Il Duce seemed safe from capture, but Skorzeny was not to be denied. A ground attack was out of the question, because of the large number of troops that would be needed, and a parachute assault would be a disaster in the thin, turbulent air. Thus, shortly after noon on September 12, a dozen German gliders poised for takeoff from Practica di Mare airfield near Rome, sweating out an Allied bombing raid. When the all clear sounded, the glider train took off, circled up through a cloud layer and set course for Gran Sasso. Half the machines became lost, but Skorzeny's glider soon was bouncing through the rough mountain air. He drew his knife and slashed a hole in the glider's fabric to look out; directly below lay Gran Sasso.

"Release! Release!" Skorzeny shouted to his pilot. A sudden jar, and all was deathly quiet, only the whistling of wind over fabric wings, as the glider spiraled into the awesome valley, toward a tiny triangle of land Skorzeny picked for a landing field. As they came closer, they saw it was a steep hillside! Skorzeny's orders were to abandon the mission if a safe landing was impossible, and glide down to the valley below, but instead he shouted to the pilot to crash land as near the hotel as possible.

Miraculously, the glider weaved and twisted through a narrow defile, and at the last second slammed to earth, jolting over large boulders that virtually tore it apart. Skorzeny leaped from the wreckage carrying an automatic weapon and sprinted toward the hotel, followed by an Italian officer he'd brought along as a decoy.

From an upstairs window, the haggard face of Mussolini appeared. He stared incredulously, then spotted the Italian officer; these were men come to liberate him and deliver him to the Allies! "Don't shoot!" he cried to his guards. Skorzeny at that moment was sprinting past a stunned *carabinieri* into a doorway, where a radioman sat tapping a transmitter key. Skorzeny kicked his chair from under him, smashed the radio with his gun butt, then raced on along a ten-foot wall.

The other gliders were crash-landing as Skorzeny scaled the wall and dashed around a corner to the main entrance. He leaped headlong at two men sitting beside a machine gun, upset them, and dashed inside the crowded lobby, filled with Italian soldiers. Taken by surprise, they stepped back as the wild-eyed Austrian commando charged up a flight of stairs. He turned a corner and shoved open a door. There stood Mussolini. By this time reinforcements had arrived from the other gliders; Skorzeny called for the garrison commander.

"You have 60 seconds to surrender," Skorzeny snapped, when an Italian colonel appeared. The colonel abruptly left, returning almost immediately with a goblet of wine. "To a gallant victor," he smiled.

Mussolini, by now aware that his captors were Germans, thrust out his jaw, straightened his rumpled uniform and cried: "I knew my friend Adolf Hitler would not abandon me! I embrace my liberator!"

By nightfall Il Duce was safely in Vienna, after a wild ride in a small Storch spotter plane that had managed to land amidst the wrecked gliders and take off with Mussolini and Skorzeny, a miracle in itself. Like Napoleon, Il Duce had his Hundred Days, as titular head of the Republican Fascist Party, until he was once more captured, and this time executed, by Italian partisans.

Another little-known war story is that of an outstanding woman glider pilot, petite, Hannah Reitsch, who started gliding at Grunau in 1932, at one time held all the world women's records for height, duration, and distance, and became first to win the coveted Silver C badge. Hans Jacobs had built to her measurements a small version of his superb *Rhonsperber* sailplane, and until the war she was among the most active of the Wasserkuppe soaring pilots.

95

Hannah Reitsch, noted prewar German sailplane champion, became test pilot of Hitler's secret Reichenberg V-1 squadron, the KG-200 Suicide Korps, who were ordered to dive to their deaths at Allied invasion fleet on D-Day.

In August, 1943, Hannah Reitsch was summoned to attend a top-secret luncheon at the Berlin Flying Club, with Luftwaffe Lieutenant Heinrich Lange, himself an experienced glider pilot, and Dr. Theo Bensinger, director of the Institute for Medical Aeronautics at Rechlin. She was told that Dr. Walter Georgii, director of the German Aeronautical Council, had ordered a secret new aircraft built around an Argus-Schmitt pulsejet engine. It was the *Vergeltungswaffe* 1, (V-1) a hush-hush effort called *Project Reichenberg*. Eighty former glider pilots had signed pledges to join the KG-200 Suicide Korps, to crash explosive-laden *Reichenbergs* into the Allied invasion fleet, when it came. Hannah, because of her reputation as a glider pilot and her small size, was asked to serve as a test pilot with the weird squadron.

96

Her first pulsejet experience was with the new Me 328 bomber, and she did not fly the *Reichenberg* machine until after six project pilots, one after the other, had mysteriously crashed to their deaths. Finally the day arrived, and Hannah buckled her small, 100-pound body into the *Reichenberg* cockpit, calmly running her eyes over the small instrument panel. She glanced through the plexiglass windscreen and waved at the pilot of the drop ship to which the *Reichenberg* was attached, as she had waited to be towed skyward in her sport gliding days. Her gloved fingers touched the control stick, and for a moment trembled. Her apprenhension passed, and as they roared off the runway, Hannah Reitsch wanted to sing. She felt a part of the deadly machine. No black box could have the sensitivity of her nerves, her muscles, her brain. Born to fly, she knew she could tame the wild ship that had killed six men.

"Prepare to release!" came the intercom voice of the Heinkel's commander. "And good luck, Hannah!"

She yanked the release handle, felt the craft drop away in free flight. There was a moment of exhilaration. She flipped on the engine switch. A throbbing wop-wop-wop-wop-wop of the pulsejet pounded in her ears. She felt herself pressed back in her seat. Gingerly she eased back on the control stick, felt the *Reichenberg* zoom skyward. She gently pressed the stick sideways, felt the ship quickly roll. Horizon and sky spun across her vision. For a moment Hannah forgot that death lurked in the sky with the slightest over-control. Her eyes blazed with excitement as she pulled through a sweeping loop, came diving earthward with a freedom she'd never experienced in flight before, not even in her sleek little *Sperber Junior* sailplane.

A second later, the *Reichenberg* was shaking violently, a wild buffeting that tore the control stick from her fingers and bruised her knees. For one terrified moment she watched rivets tearing loose from the wings. She throttled down the flow of fuel, eased out of the screaming dive, and climbed through a gentle Immelmann turn to kill off her airspeed. The vibration dampened, and stopped.

Laughing now, Hannah stunted above the test field at Rechlin, while on the ground, others of the Suicide Korps gasped. Darting across the heavens, the V-1, under her professional touch, was a thing of the future. The pulsejet engine finally coughed and quit; she heard only the whine of wind as she once again flew as a glider pilot. Back on earth, the others

Hannah Reitsch in the cockpit of V-1 Reichenberg suicide ship, which became the *Buzz Bomb*. Above her head is Argus-Schmitt pulse-jet engine.

crowded about with open admiration, and listened with a new respect when she described the problem and its solution.

"Some day we'll be flying faster than sound," she told them. "But now, we must fly carefully when we get close to sonic speed. We will need Dr. Georgii's wind tunnels to learn what is happening."

In the closing days of the war, there was no time to perfect the *Reichenberg* machine. In the face of advancing Allied troops, hundreds of unmanned V-1's were catapulted toward London in an 80-day horror attack; the weapons were derisively called *Doodle Bugs* and *Buzz Bomb*s by the British. The KG-200 Suicide Korps glider pilots, who might have flown the *Reichenbergs* in screaming death dives against the Allied invasion fleet, instead were committed to fly Focke Wulf 190's.

The coming of D-Day interrupted yet another unusual glider program. Working in shifts, four hours a day for ten months, a group of British war prisoners, confined to Colditz Castle in Germany, constructed a two-place "escape" glider in a concealed attic workshop. They secretly fashioned a craft they called the *Colditz Cock,* from any materials they could scrounge. Wings were covered with bed sheets, doped with boiled milk; control surfaces were attached with cupboard hinges. A 60-foot catapult launch track made from mess tables was to straddle the ridge of the tile roof, and a two-ton bag of rocks, tied to a rope, dropped to provide launch power. Amazed Yankee invasion troops were shown the strange bird by the proud POW's, who never got the chance to use her, perhaps fortunately. The story came to light in an article in the British publication *Air Review,* authored by the project's leader, Flight Lieutenant L.J.E. Finch.

98

Royal Air Force air armada of gliders and tow planes lined up for takeoff for liberation of Europe on D-Day, June 6, 1944.

Shortly after 1 A.M. on June 6, 1944, the long awaited D-Day invasion of Normandy got under way. Lieutenant Colonel M.C. (Mike) Murphy, a prewar stunt flyer who had thrilled crowds at the National Air Races in Cleveland, Ohio, climbed into the left seat of a Waco glider on the line at England's Aldermaston Field, waved reassuringly to the airborne troopers in back, and called the tow pilot, Colonel William B. Whitacre. "All set here, tug," Colonel Murphy said. At precisely 1:19 A.M. the C-47 began to roll; Murphy felt the 300-foot nylon towline tighten. The Waco, *Fighting Falcon,* a gift from students of Greenville, Michigan, lifted into the air, the first glider to depart for the coast of France.

Unlike the Sicily glider invasion, the mission of the Wacos over Normandy was one of aerial reinforcement rather than initial strike. The first glider tows, primarily artillery airlifts, were two night missions, coded *Chicago* and *Detroit.* Mike Murphy's *Fighting Falcon* was the first of 52 gliders of *Chicago,* which airlifted Batteries A and B of the 81st Airborne AA Battalion. The takeoff was timed to reach the landing zone, on the Contentin Peninsula, at 4 A.M., shortly before dawn. Despite the lesson of Sicily, the danger from Nazi gunfire was considered greater than the risk of night landings in small fields studded with ten-inch poles set up by the defenders, and called "Rommel's asparagus."

The flight across the Channel at first went uneventfully for the *Chicago* group, though one glider, carrying a special radio set for the 101st Division, broke loose and landed in England. Another tow pilot straggled out of formation, and released his glider short of the LZ (landing zone), but the other 49 towplanes, flying under a bright moon, arrived six minutes ahead of schedule and cut loose their Wacos at 450 feet altitude.

99

Those last 450 feet were the toughest—groping down through semi-darkness, the glider pilots did a remarkable job, crash landing in small fields. Some ran into trouble, including a Waco whose personnel included Brigadier General Don F. Pratt, assistant commander of the 101st Division, who had joined the glider serial as an afterthought. General Pratt was one of five airborne troops killed in crash landings. Mike Murphy's glider skidded across a damp field and smashed into a tree; with both legs fractured, he crawled to a nearby ditch and spent the day shooting at German troops with a submachine gun. Later, he was flown back to England, the first American casualty evacuated from France.

Shortly after the *Chicago* mission left England, the *Detroit* serial of 52 Wacos, towed by as many C-47's, left Ramsbury and headed for the Cotentin. Encountering a cloud bank over the French coast, the glider pilots could not event see their tow planes; in the obscurity seven gliders broke loose or were released. Breaking free of the cloud bank, the others flew on, low enough to suffer numerous casualties from ground fire. Only 37 pilots reached their LZ. While the *Detroit* glider drop fared better than the Lanbroke disaster at Sicily, rows of "Rommel's asparagus" tore up many Wacos, and one ran into a startled herd of cattle. Three troops were killed and 23 injured, and though several *Jeeps* broke loose, the gliders delivered intact more than half a dozen anti-tank guns, which quickly went into action on the outskirts of St. Mere Eglise.

British and American troop and cargo gliders crashed side by side in French pasture where they landed airborne infantry on D-Day.

The third D-Day glider mission, *Keokuk,* was the first daylight operation, leaving Aldermaston two hours before sunset on what turned out to be a virtual milk run. Thirty-two Horsas carried 157 men, 40 vehicles, six guns, and 19 tons of supplies for the 101st Division; two landed within German lines and were captured, but crash landings were few. Enemy gunfire killed 14 troops and injured another 30, but the mission still proved daylight glider landings preferrable to night landings.

Following *Keokuk* came a sundown mission, *Elmira,* split into two serials of 76 and 100 Wacos and Horsas, which crossed the Utah invasion beach under a heavy fighter escort. A severe problem faced them on landing; the fields were less than 200 yards long and were surrounded by high trees; many were flooded, or studded with poles. Typical was the landing of Captain William W. Bates; unable to reach a large field, he chose a small one, lowered flaps and landed at 70 miles an hour. His glider bounced twice and plunged through a row of trees, which stripped off the wing and landing gear. Enemy fire ripped the tail to shreds, but the only casualty was a soldier who broke his leg as a result of leaving his safety belt unfastened. The cargo, an ammunition trailer, was unloaded intact within 20 minutes.

*Elmira's* second echelon encountered intense ground fire that killed or wounded numerous men in the short time it took to glide to earth. Many Horsa pilots, despite strict orders to land slowly, slammed into the small fields at 100 miles an hour; only 13 of 84 Horsas landed intact. Ten of the 196 glider pilots on this mission were killed, 29 wounded, seven reported missing.

Two other glider missions took place during the Normandy invasion, on D-Day plus 1—*Galveston* and *Hackensack. Galveston* came in at daybreak south of Utah beach, a low-level run. The troop gliders cut loose virtually on the deck, decreasing exposure to enemy fire but increasing the risk of a landing crash. During *Hackensack,* glider release was raised to 600 feet, and the comparatively inexperienced 441st Group turned in a near perfect performance, picking and choosing their fields and landing with few casualties and cargoes near intact.

Of 1,030 American glider pilots who reached Normandy, all but 197 were accounted for. These received a commendation from General Matthew B. Ridgeway, for their good service.

Of passing interest is the fact that Robert Kronfeld, the Wasserkuppe

Here, one can see the giant size of the British Horsa troop glider.

birdman who first crossed the English Channel by glider, became a British subject and test-flew Horsas as a squadron leader with the Airborne Forces Experimental Establishment. Kronfeld was killed in the crash of a GAL-56 experimental tailless glider, in 1956.

Inside Fortress Europe, glider forces played other important and still more effective combat and supply roles. Typical was the story of squadron leader Captain Jacque Boyle, whose serial of 35 Wacos went into the Arnheim sector in two waves. In the first wave, which he led, one glider pilot was killed. The second wave ended with all but one pilot dead. Boyle flew a total of five missions, an unusually high number. On his second landing, in the Rhine Valley, he found his target field bristling with AA guns. He managed to divert to another field at the last moment, and escaped into the woods, where he watched the Germans catch the next glider wave in a murderous crossfire.

Howard Cowan, an Associated Press war correspondent, recalled the agony of a glider landing inside Germany, at the end of a three-hour tow behind a C-47: "You shake hands with the others and glue your eyes on the pilot, waiting for him to push the lever to cut the glider loose from the tow plane. Bursts of rifle fire are accompanied now by the popping of machine guns and a gutteral whommph of 88-mm shells. You unconsciously lift off your seat and brace as if to meet hot metal singing through the smoke. You find yourself dodging and weaving from something you can't even see.

"Then the pilot's hand goes up and forward.

" 'Going down!' he shouts, and the nose pitches forward steeply. The speed slackens and the roar of the wind dies down and the battle noises suddenly are magnified into a terrifying din.

" 'Now,' says the Sergeant, 'is when you pray.'

"The right wing tilts sharply as the shadow of another glider flits past. It almost hits us.

"Smoke is thick and acrid—like being inside a burning house. You can see half a dozen buildings aflame on the ground. Dozens of gliders are parked at crazy angles on every field. Everyone with a weapon has it cocked and across his lap.

"Then, before you know it, the ground is racing underneath. You are in a pasture, crashing through a fence, bounding across a gully, clipping a tree with a wingtip. You've made it—landed and nobody hurt.

"You relax for a moment, but realize a split second later that was a mistake. Bullets are ripping through the glider.

" 'Get outa here! Get outa here!' someone shouts, and prayers give way to curses as first one and then the other kicks savagely at the door. You're getting shot at from a house at the other end of the meadow.

"You roll into a shallow ditch. A foot of red, slimy water makes no difference. It actually feels good trickling down the open throat of your woolen shirt and filtering into the toes of your boots, and you're tempted to drink it, for your mouth is parched. . . ."

Hundreds of Waco CG-4A gliders used in the invasion of Holland were later repaired for use in an assault on the Rhone Valley.

And well it should have been; the massive glider assault on the Rhine Valley near Wesel stood as the greatest airborne invasion in history, with 40,000 troops participating. By now, glider airborne strikes were running smoothly; of 2,046 gliders and aircraft dispatched by the U.S. IX Troop Carrier Command, 2,029 accomplished their missions successfully.

The green Wacos and the big Horsas were used again in southern France, during Operation Dragoon, when more than 2,000 troops of the 550th Glider Infantry Battalion were airlifted from Italy to invade the French Riviera, in hundreds of Wacos sweeping over in wave after wave. They came so fast that at one time four waves arrived simultaneously, forcing the glider pilots to dodge and weave to avoid midair collisions. Once again they encountered rows of "Rommel's asparagus" and diverted to other fields, most already filled with crash-landed Wacos. Few gliders escaped damage, and 11 glider pilots lost their lives, but the operation, code named *Dove,* was a tactical success.

Glider warfare played a significant role in the defeat of the Japanese forces in the China-Burma-India theater of operations in 1944, under perhaps the worst flying weather ever encountered by motorless combat aircraft. With the war in Europe drawing to a close, Allied forces turned full attention on East Asia. A total of 342 CG-4A and CG-13 troop-cargo gliders were shipped in crates to the CBI theater, another 600 were made available through British lend-lease.

Heading for the French Riviera landing zone between Cannes and Toulon, C-47's tow CG-4A's of 12th Air Force Troop Carrier Air Division, 1944.

Gliders over The Hump. This remarkable operation took place on March 5, 1944, when First Air Commando Force flew British troops 200 miles behind Japanese lines to capture tiny Myitkyina Airfield.

Curiously enough, army mules were high-priority passengers on one unforgettable mission deep behind enemy lines, led by Colonel John R. Alison of the First Commando Force. Alison, an American fighter ace with seven victories, had never flown a glider until the afternoon of March 5, 1945; after a short check flight he led a night takeoff to begin a 3¼ hour tow from India across northern Burma, into a remote area of China 200 miles behind Japanese lines. To reach their goal, a tiny clearing called Myitkyina Airfield, the gliders had to cross a high range of mountains along the Salween River, a notoriously frightful air corridor, The Hump.

On that flight went hundreds of "Chindit" jungle guerrilla fighters of British General Orde Wingate, plus mules, bulldozers, trailers, tractors, graders, scrapers, electric generators, and lights—everything needed to carve an airstrip from the jungle. Groping through the turbulent night sky without lights was only a prelude to trouble—once the first wave of gliders reached their objective they piled into each other on landing and crashed into trees and fallen logs, killing 23 men and injuring 60. Colonel Alison,

A Chinese soldier stands guard over the equipment-loaded gliders a few hours after Myitkyina Airfield had been recaptured from the Japanese in a daring night assault.

fearing the landing would turn into a disaster, tried to radio a warning to aircraft still flying. The field radio had been damaged in landing, and the operator could only get out one word, the wrong one at that—the code word for *disaster*. Back in India, General Wingate and Colonel Phil Cochran, commander of the First Air Commandos, heard the word and were shocked. Not until morning did they learn that more than 100 gliders had reached their objective and construction crews were bulldozing a big airstrip. By 7:20 P.M. that night, the first Troop Carrier Command DC-3's were landing, and Myitkyina was secured.

If getting gliders into remote areas was difficult, getting them out was more so. During the airborne invasion of Holland, General Arnold insisted that every effort be made to retrieve the Wacos and after three months' hard work by 900 technicians, 281 rickety, badly weathered CG-4A's were flown to troop carrier bases near Chartres. The method employed for the glider pickups was developed before the war by Richard C. du Pont, as an operational technique for All American Aviation, a pioneer air mail carrier of which he was president. On October 23, 1942, du Pont first demonstrated his system to military officials, using a Piper glider conversion. Basically, the retrieval equipment was a rework of a large aircraft wheel and brake assembly, to change it into a reel carrying several hundred feet of line. The line was threaded through a hook, which dropped from the rear of the tow airplane to pick up a cable looped between two poles on the ground, with the glider between. By this system, a flying DC-3 could jerk a CG-4A off the ground smoothly from a dead stop. Used both in Europe and in the CBI theater to recover wounded men from battlefields, the retrieval system proved successful, and saved many lives getting men to hospitals in minutes instead of hours.

Perhaps the most dramatic World War II glider retrieval occurred in the early summer of 1945 in a remote, high valley in the mountains of New Guinea. Air Force Lieutenant Colonel Phil W. Garrison remembered the hidden valley as "a flat piece of ground at about 14,000 to 18,000 feet up in the Oranje Mountains, surrounded by cliffs that reached up to 24,000 feet." Inaccessible by ground due to the sheer walls surrounding it, the valley became a place of great interest to Colonel Ray T. Elsmore, a Troop Carrier Command wing commander, who found it. Unable to land because of the high altitude and cliffs, Colonel Elsmore made numerous reconnaissance flights into the valley, in his personal plushed-up B-25, to photograph the natives, a stone-age people living in complete isolation.

"It became something of a local tourist attraction," recalled Colonel Garrison, who was assigned to make wire-recorded narrations from the plexiglass nose of the B-25. "Elsmore's outfit ran Special Services flights up there in C-47 *Gooney Birds,* for the amusement and amazement of his troops."

On one such flight on May 13, 1945, with 26 aboard, storm clouds suddenly closed in, trapping the C-47 inside the valley. In trying to climb out, the pilot struck a peak, scattering wreckage over the mountainside. All but three aboard died. The survivors were WAC Corporal Margaret Hastings, Lieutenant Robert McCollom, and T/Sgt. Kenneth Decker. All were seriously injured, with second degree burns and fractures. For two nights they wandered through the three-mile-high rain forest, more dead than alive. By following a river, they came to a clearing, and there awaited rescue.

Primitive tribesmen armed with stone axes appeared. The natives turned out to be friendly, but were of little help. Search planes located the trio on the third day, and dropped emergency supplies, until some way could be figured to rescue them. Weeks passed, during which paramedics para-

A Douglas C-47 tow plane, in one of the most delicate air operations, snatches a glider off the ground at Asansol, India, September, 1944.

chuted in to administer to their wounds, and at Hollandia Air Force Base officers argued over the best way to bring them out. Scaling the cliffs was virtually impossible; Seabees offered to airlift in bulldozers and steel runway mats, but landing a DC-3 at 18,000 feet on a short field was out of the question. Helicopters were only beginning to appear in the South Pacific, and not one was available. Finally, Colonel Elsmore suggested a glider pickup; the system was then being used in Burma. Practice runs were made at a small offshore island called Wakde.

Garrison: "Day after day we'd fly out to Wakde and witness the hairraising attempts of the C-47 and CG-4A crews to become proficient at this nerve-wracking procedure. This went on for some time and nobody got dead—not even hurt—a circumstance that can be attributed to Divine Providence more than to the training methods. Finally, they got one flawless test snatch and decided to call it proficiency."

Meanwhile, back in Shangri-La, paratroopers dropped in and built a glider strip, erected a snatch rig and set up a base camp with a private boudoir for Corporal Hastings, from a yellow nylon parachute. Finally, on June 28, the CG-4A glider, *Leaking Louise,* sailed down into the valley and settled onto the runway. The pilot, Lieutenant Henry E. Paver, yelled: "This express takes off in 30 minutes! All aboard!"

The three survivors bid farewell to their native friends and climbed aboard, carrying stone axes, bows and arrows for souveniers. The pickup plane swooped into the valley, with Colonel Garrison following in the plexiglass nose of Colonel Elsmore's B-25, lounging in a big, red-leather swivel chair, microphone on and recorder turning. As he reported the action, the C-47 latched onto the glider rope and jerked it up through the treetops, finally breaking clear. The survivors landed at Hollandia 90 minutes later, ending their 47-day adventure, and soon *Leaking Louise* went back to retrieve the other rescuers.

Glad to be alive, Corporal Hastings was met by reporters and photographers and told them what had happened, including something the glider pilot, Lieutenant Paver had said when she'd asked what would happen if the tow rope broke.

"Well," Paver replied, "the Army's got me insured for ten thousand dollars!"

The awesome Sierra Wave. This view, taken from 36,000 feet, looks South along Owens Valley and the Sierra Nevada Range. Winds from the right accompanies a Pacific storm blowing over the mountains, depositing snow on top and sweeping down in a *foehnwall* to scour the valley floor with blowing dust at 50 knots. Wind then rises in a steep shearline, lifting dust into dangerous roll cloud (left), so violent it can tear wings from a sailplane.

# 7/TO THE STRATOSPHERE

In December of 1951, an unprecedented series of storms ranged across northern California, forcing the closing of Golden Gate Bridge for the first time, flooding San Joaquin Valley in drenching rain, and stalling the streamliner *City of San Francisco* in historic Donner Pass as deep snow covered the Sierra Nevada range with an early white mantle. The blame was placed on an errant polar jet stream that swung far south of its normal winter storm track.

Concerned weather observers on December 18 watched a large, dark, roll cloud form at dawn over Owens Valley, an arid basin below the Sierra's eastern scarp. Above it arched two decks of high lenticular clouds, marking the cap of a lee mountain wave; a third "lennie" formed over the Inyo Mountains east of the valley, marking a second wave. Low scud and blowing snow trailed in a cloudfall far down the rugged east wall of the Sierras, while throughout the day, the stratospheric lenticular *foehnwall* hung steady and unmoving, its downwash resembling water overflowing a dam.

On hand to study this classic mountain wave system were experts of year-old Project Sierra Wave, government and civilian meteorologists from the Air Weather Service, U.S. Weather Bureau, UCLA, and the Naval Ordnance Test Station at Inyokern. Sponsors of the Project were the Geophysics Research Directorate of the USAF's Cambridge Research Center, and the Office of Naval Research. Their goal was to learn what they could of mountain wave phenomena, held responsible for an alarming number of plane crashes in stormy weather. To bring back further data, glider pilots of the Southern California Soaring Association were enlisted to fly inside the Sierra Wave itself.

The author was invited to participate in a Sierra Wave flight with Harland Ross, a fixed base operator at Bishop Airport, and quickly accepted for personal reasons—Owens Valley had been my training ground in light

111

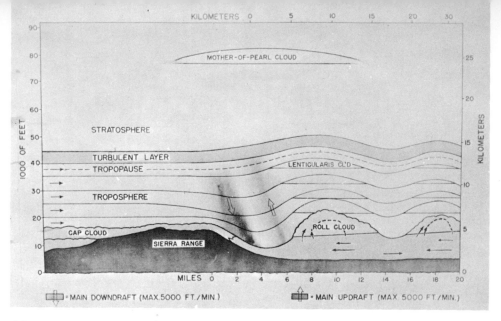

The structure of a mountain lee-wave system, showing location of dangerous roll cloud downwind of range, and lenticularis cloud caps.

planes, and I well remembered encountering tremendous lift which sucked up tons of sand and tumbleweeds that soared thousands of feet into dark rotor clouds boiling overhead. On one such day I managed to spin an S1A Interstate Cadet through twenty turns and lose only 500 feet!

Ross and I climbed into his modified Schweizer TG-3, bundled up in Arctic flying gear and equipped with oxygen. Our tow plane, a BT-13, was piloted by Bob Symons, a local flier employed by a power company to seed clouds with dry ice from a P-38, and so increase snow cover in the Bishop Cups watershed area. Symons knew the Sierra Wave well, and in it had frequently soared his converted eight-ton World War II fighter, with both engines stopped, for more than an hour at a time. So, here we go:

At 15,000 feet we top the snowy crest of Mt. Whitney, and climb higher toward the *altocumulus lenticularis* arching across the sky. North and south, as far as we can see, is the snow-capped Sierra range. West to the Pacific stretches a sea of cottony stratus. To the east, parallel to the Sierras and above us, extends a black, ominous roll cloud formation.

"Check your fingernails!" Ross shouts back.

I can barely hear his voice, because of his oxygen mask and the crisp, rarefied air. I slip off my gloves and study my nails. They're all there, none blue. Sierra Wave riders are alert to the swift danger of anoxia—lack of oxygen—that can knock you unconscious before you know it. An early warning is blueness of the nails. I remember the fate of Karl Erik Oevgaard, a Swedish soaring pilot who went up seeking a solo altitude record in the Sierra Wave. He failed to return alive, but his fate was revealed in a roll of film found in the wreckage of his sailplane. A picture of the panel showed he had reached 30,000 feet, and something else—the oxygen pressure gauge read quite low. The next picture on the roll, an exterior shot of the Sierras, was badly out of focus, although Oevgaard was an excellent photographer. The last picture, taken at 32,000 feet, showed the glider still climbing, and the oxygen pressure at zero.

The variometer on the rear instrument panel says we are climbing at 2,000 feet a minute. The sensitive altimeter needle is sweeping around and around, like a broken clock. We're climbing fast, riding the smooth updraft beneath the leading edge of the roll cloud. I glance up through the plexiglass canopy, am startled to see we're about to plunge into the roll cloud. Ross's helmeted head turns anxiously as he studies it.

"Hang on!" he yells, in that faint, faraway voice. "It's gonna get rough!"

No sooner has he spoken than something hammers our glider with the force of a sledgehammer. I'm shoved hard against my safety belt; my head strikes the canopy, an ivory-headed bullet. My oxygen mask slips off. I bite my lip to keep from sucking the brittle air rushing in through the hole my head made. Ross fights the controls, and we shoot out through the top of the roll cloud. Suddenly all is ghostly still again. The thundering silence of the stratosphere is fantastic, unreal. As it presses in, I wonder at the power of this mighty wave we're riding like an elevator.

Series of lenticular (lens-shaped) clouds marking tops of atmospheric waves downstream from the Sierra Nevada.

This is what happened to Larry Edgar's sailplane when he inadvertently entered a roll cloud; the wings of the plane were ripped off, and Edgar himself floated for half an hour inside the cloud in his chute.

Harland Ross (front) and George Diebert prepare for Sierra Wave ride, to 36,100 feet, in converted TG-3 Schweizer sailplane.

It was such pioneer flying by Ross and Symons that first unlocked the secret of the Sierra Wave, and the way Pacific cold fronts dump their moisture as they sweep over the 14,000-foot peaks to spill into Owens Valley, becoming hot and dry *foehn* winds by adiabatic compression. On the valley floor, the winds pick up debris and hurl it high in a rolling motion, like curling spray at the foot of a waterfall. The roll cloud holds the greatest danger—unpredictable turbulence that can snap a glider's wings like matchsticks. Above the roll cloud, glassy smooth stratospheric wind may form a secondary wave, capped with its own lenticular. Succeeding waves may extend downwind for hundreds of miles.

Suddenly we are inside the Sierra Wave itself, and although Ross has the glider's nose pointed downward, we're shooting toward the stratosphere in an uprushing air wave that carries us toward the lenticular, spreading its wings like a beautiful banner, pink with sunset glow. As we pass 22,000 feet, I remember a record flight made by Ross and George Deibert, in the same TG-3 we are flying. On January 27, 1950, Ross and Deibert worked their way south past Mt. Whitney, passing 28,000 feet, high enough to qualify for a world two-place absolute altitude record. As the lift was strong, they continued climbing, and at 29,600 feet passed Fred Walters' national record of 18,100 feet gained. Soon they passed 30,000 feet, exceeding Guy Rousselet and Leon Faivre's record gain of 22,244 feet, made in France. At 26,100 feet above sea level the lift ended for Ross and Deibert; their feet nearly frozen, they headed home. Their height was surpassed on December 30, 1950, by William S. Ivans, Jr., a San Diego missile engineer, who climbed the Sierra Wave to 42,100 feet for a world single-place sailplane record. Two other Sierra Wave Project pilots, Larry Edgar and Harold Kleiforth, on March 19, 1952, raised the two-place record to 44,255 feet, and in 1961 Paul Bikle, Director of the NASA Flight Research Center at Edwards Air Force Base, reached an incredible summit altitude of 46,267 feet in a Schweizer 1-23E (the story of this remarkable flight is told in the next chapter).

Cold air streaming into the TG-3's cockpit through the cracked canopy finally forces Ross and me to turn back; isothermic temperatures of -69° F exist in the stratosphere, and we're not dressed for that. On the way home we dive through clear air ahead of the dangerous roll cloud, and slant down toward Bishop Airport.

Over a cup of hot coffee, Ross showed me a report of a remarkable glider tow, made by Larry Edgar beneath a rotor cloud, in which turbulence was so severe it was impossible for him to stay in level flight. On one occasion, the sailplane shot ahead of the towplane, narrowly avoiding a collision, and the tow line looped back over the sailplane's wings and canopy. "Before I could release," Edgar reported, "the rope was yanked off the top of the sailplane and the slack was taken up."

On April 25, 1955, Edgar and Project pilot Dr. A.J. Kuettner, flying two sailplanes over Bishop at the same time, ran into destructive turbulence with gusts estimated at 120 feet per second. On landing, Dr. Kuettner laconically reported encountering plus 4G, minus 3G accelerations in his Schweizer 2-25: "I tried to take the speed back to 45 mph, but in spite of the nose-up attitude, speed increased rapidly to 80 mph and turbulence became so severe that I lost control. This happened when small clouds puffs formed around my ship in front of the main roll cloud. I had no other choice than to penetrate between them, while trying to descend below the base of the huge roll cloud."

Edgar, flying a Pratt-Read sailplane some distance away, heard Dr. Kuettner's voice crackle over the radio: "I'm getting fantastic turbulence!" Below him, the roll cloud seethed like a black volcano. At 17,000 feet he headed for Bishop Airport, hoping to follow Dr. Kuettner into clear air ahead of the rotor. "Instead of clear air," he reported, "a puff of cottony vapor materialized, and seem to swell up before my nose at the last moment. I looked at the needle and ball. Suddenly and instantaneously the needle went off center, then swung violently the other way. The shearing action was terrific. It forced me sideways in my seat, first to the left, then to the right. At the same time, a fantastic positive G load shoved me down into the seat. Just as I was blacking out, I felt a violent roll to the left and heard a loud explosion. I was unable to see after blacking out, but I was conscious and felt my head hit the canopy. There was a lot of noise and I was taking quite a beating. I was too stunned to attempt to bail out. Then, just as suddenly as all this violence started, it became quiet, except for the sound of wind whistling by. I felt I was falling free of all wreckage, except for something holding my feet."

Edgar was alarmed by the thought that he had fallen unconscious with the wreckage so near the ground; he reached for his parachute D-ring and pulled. "I felt the 'chute snap open, and my feet jerk free. For some time I

116

Larry Edgar being towed aloft behind a BT-13, underneath an ominous roll cloud.

swung violently, trying to piece together what happened. I'd lost my flight boots; my helmet, oxygen mask, and gloves were gone. I could hear a hissing. The hose was ripped from my bailout oxygen bottle. My vision began to clear and I saw a faint point of light, oscillating back and forth. It was the sun—I was still near the top of the cloud!"

Edgar realized he was virtually trapped inside the roll cloud, riding the hurricane updrafts in his parachute. He tried to pull on the shroud lines, to spill air and come down, but his left arm was numb, his shoulder broken. He tried with his right hand, with no better success. He checked his watch —he'd been inside the cloud ten minutes. Finally strength returned enough to slip the 'chute, down through the bottom of the roll cloud, where he saw large pieces of the wrecked glider floating upward, like autumn leaves.

His left eye was blinded, his face cold and wet with blood. Thousands of feet below, a strong surface wind scoured the valley floor with drifting snow, and overturned a bus. Another ten minutes passed before Edgar's 'chute slowly came down from the cloud. The worst of the turbulence had passed; he struck the ground hard, the wind dragging him over huge boulders. Rescuers found him dazed, but alive.

What good has come from the dramatic Sierra Wave Project?

Rather than an exercise in foolhardiness, it was a serious effort that would save many lives in the future—of both sailplane and powerplane pilots—by revealing the internal mechanism of the mountain storm systems and so advising airmen what to watch for, danger zones that appear whenever a critical arrangement of the rotor flow beneath such waves produces turbulence of destructive magnitude.

Warnings were issued to pilots to avoid mountain wave systems when the following signs appear:

1. A deep roll cloud with tops unusually high, exceeding considerably the tops of the cap cloud over the mountains.

2. A rotor cloud system with the leading edge unusually far downwind.

3. Hurricane force surface winds between the mountain range and rotor zone, carrying dust into the roll cloud.

Sierra Wave Project pilots in stratospheric gear.

4. A straight leading edge on the roll cloud, instead of one following the bends of the mountain range.

5. A rotor cloud extending far downwind without periodicity.

6. Turbulence concentrated in small cloud puffs ahead of the roll cloud's leading edge.

The Sierra Wave Project revealed another curious phenomena—frontal passages over the mountains from the northwest, accompanied by strong winds, precede distant severe weather, on the Great Plains in the lee of the Rockies, within 24 to 36 hours. If the Sierra Wave air is dry and cloudless, dry northerlies called *Chinooks* (snow-eaters) and dust storms rip across Nebraska and Kansas, but when frontal passages at Bishop are accompanied by dense clouds and some rain, thunderstorms and tornadoes may play havoc over the plains country. A classic example occurred on May 24, 1955, when a moderate lee wave appeared at Bishop with overcast, rain, and a northerly sandstorm, one day before Udall, Kansas, exploded with violent tornado activity.

Historically, mountain lee waves have been observed for centuries on the north slope of the Alps, where the name *foehn* (west) wind was first given to hot, dry air believed to come from the Sahara Desert in wintertime. Subsequent investigation by meteorologists showed they were Mediterranean winds that lost their moisture as snow over the Alps, and then were heated by compression flowing down the north slopes. This explanation, however, did not account for the strange lenticular clouds that formed ahead of fast moving storms. In Silesia, a maize farmer named Gottlieb Matz won local fame predicting such storms by watching for "lennies" that formed over mile-high Mount Schneekoppe; his name was given to the cloud—in Silesian dialect it became the famous *Moazagotl*.

By 1933, sailplanes were penetrating lee waves in the Riesengebirge Mountains of eastern Germany, and their relation to the *foehn* winds was established. Elsewhere in the world, similar mountain lee waves ultimately became favorite soaring sites. East of the Rockies, the Andes, the Appalachians, and other north-south mountain systems, such waves will form when cold fronts cross from the west or northwest. In New Zealand, the famed North West Arch, which forms over and beyond Christchurch and hangs stationary at 30,000 feet, has been described by the noted soaring pilot, Philip Wills, as a cloud whose leading edge, stretching out of sight to the north, "has the curious guazy definition of all wave clouds. Its underside is

Altocumulus clouds in rows mark upper "streets" of thermal activity.

heavy with pendulous bulges, and is streaked and serrated like a monster construction of multi-plywood. In the rising sun it shines out in the still, dark sky a ruby red."

The thrill of flying through a *foehnwall* was described to the author by Hannes Linke, a skillful soaring pilot who came to America after learning to fly in 1956 at Kaufbeuren, Bavaria. In 1958, when he was twenty, Linke won his Silver Badge and glider instructor rating—the youngest in Germany to do so—and for two years instructed at a North Sea glider base on the Isle of Juist. Linke won his coveted Diamond Badge at Innsbruck, Austria, in 1960, reaching 27,000 feet altitude from a winch tow release at 800 feet. The big day came on October 23, 1960, after a late party, at which Hannes was helping members of a soaring club celebrate other successes. At 5 A.M. his alarm went off. He sleepily called the weather station; a strong *foehn* was blowing.

"I hurried to the field, where others had my glider ready—it was my turn to fly—and I quickly finished the paperwork, sealed my barograph and filled my oxygen bottle. There were some 60 sailplanes up when I released.

120

I thermaled to 7,000 feet, at the base of a huge cap cloud on top of the mountain. For a while I just sat there, thermaling with dive brakes out to stay beneath it, until I could adjust my oxygen mask and artificial horizon. Then I went into the cloud and came out on top, 4,500 feet higher still.

"Above the top of the cap cloud was the *foehnwall*, a kind of thick lenticular whose front, or upwind edge formed a sheer cliff, perhaps 3,000 feet high. I flew back along the top of the cap cloud, like ridge soaring, and then along the base of the *foehnwall*, wondering what to do next. I'd never flown in such strong air before.

"Suddenly I was in it! The *foehnwall* was dark inside, and I groped my way on instruments, turned and flew ahead into the wind, toward the knife-sharp leading edge of the *foehnwall*. I inched the nose of my glider out into the sunlit sky and sat there, at perhaps 50 miles an hour, half in and half out of cloud, looking down the dizzying sheer wall!

"I had no maps with me, and the problem I now faced was not how to gain altitude and win my Diamond, but how to get back down. I went over the top of the *foehnwall*, and found a hole in the lower cloud deck downwind of the valley. I could not come down there and return to Innsbruck, so once more I penetrated the *foehnwall*, flew through it on instruments, and crossed to the other side of the valley. From there I descended through half a dozen cloud layers, extended my dive brakes and glided back to land. I'd been up one hour ten minutes."

Linke considered the *foehnwall* a nice place to visit by sailplane, but for action he preferred California's Mojave Desert region. "Cross-country flying is the real challenge in soaring today," he explained. "In southern California you have a selection of desert thermals, slope winds, marine air discontinuities, and mountain waves to choose from." By utilizing such elemental forces in the Mojave sky, Linke flew a world record flight over a 100-kilometer triangle, an adventure described in the following chapter.

On April 1, 1960, wave soaring got an unexpected dividend from outer space; Tiros I, the world's first meteorological satellite, was launched into a 400-mile orbit to demonstrate the feasibility of using slow-scan TV cameras aboard a gyroscopically spin-stabilized satellite. On its first orbit, historic televised pictures revealed how upper air atmospheric waves are generated downwind from gigantic mountain barriers such as the Rockies and the Andes. These mountains, it was discovered, served as primary anchors in the planetary wave pattern of the westerlies.

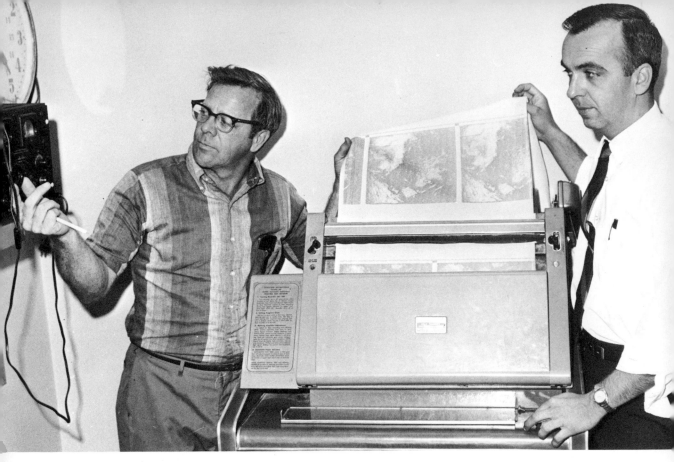

Dan Dibble, UCLA technician (left), built this "junkyard" receiver to receive APT (automatic picture transmission) photos of world weather from satellites, to help soaring pilots locate wave clouds.

Until Tiros, only an occasional visual observation, or the packing of isobars along mountain crests on synoptic weather charts, provided any kind of forecast for mountain wave prediction. By the time these were available to soaring pilots, the waves were long gone. Tiros I supplied exciting pictures of large wave patterns, but it still took up to six hours to assemble the photographs into composite sketches (called nephanalyses) for transmission on the national weather facsimile network.

In December, 1963, something appeared to give soaring pilots a still more valuable new weather prediction service—virtually instantaneous cloud cover photos from a device carried into orbit by Tiros VIII—the APT (Automatic Picture Transmission) system. With APT, anybody on earth could receive weather pictures from space, but unfortunately, the cost of a receiving antenna, amplifier, FM receiver, and facsimile recording equipment ran to about $40,000.

At UCLA, an ingenious lab technician, Dan Dibble, in the tradition of Mark Twain, did something about the weather instead of talking about it. He visited local surplus electronic stores and junkyards, and bought an assortment of gadgets. He bolted together a secondhand ham aerial, with the parts at right angles to compensate for the satellite's tumbling; it cost $100 and looked like the smashed grill on a Stutz Bearcat. Next he picked up a used Hallicrafter receiver for $100 and fixed it to tune in the frequency of another weather satellite with APT capability—ESSA II. A $50 amplifier, an old voltmeter, and an antenna tuner completed the inventory, except for the facsimile recorder. He found one gathering dust in the UCLA attic.

When he got his machine hooked up and the first pictures came in, they didn't match those from the Weather Bureau. He discovered the machine was polarized, so that clouds appeared black and the ground white. "I was getting anti-clouds," Dibble grinned. "The snow on top of the Sierras looked black, and that showed me what was wrong." Finally he was able to receive good pictures of large scale mountain wave systems, covering an area of 1,000 miles on a side, within five minutes of the time they were taken. Such information could be relayed immediately to soaring sites, and even to pilots in the air, to direct them to the best waves.

The first mountain wave photographed by Tiros I, on April 18, 1960, showed a remarkably regular and widespread pattern extending some 200 miles downwind from the Andes in South America. In 1963 and 1964, thanks to the enterprise of a top Washington, D.C. weather forecaster who was also a soaring pilot, Tiros photos of mountain waves were for the first time compared with actual wave flights, to get the big picture of the kind of weather the pilots were flying in. The expert was Charles V. Lindsay, of the Environmental Science Services Administration (ESSA) Washington Forecast Center. Although the pilots were unaware of the experiment, it was a revealing study.

On June 6, 1964, soaring pilot Bruce Beebe won his Diamond Badge in a wave after releasing over Reno, Nevada, at 6,600 feet. He lost about 300 feet, then soared in the wave to 23,500 feet for a gain in excess of 17,000 feet, in the lee of the Sierra Nevadas. A nephanalysis made from a Tiros VIII photograph showed wave clouds extending another 400 miles downwind and 330 miles along the mountain slope. Beebe made a long

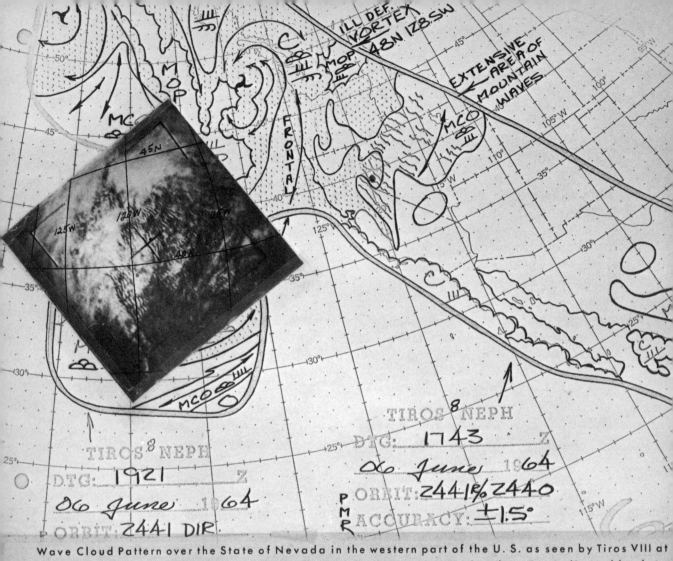

Wave Cloud Pattern over the State of Nevada in the western part of the U. S. as seen by Tiros VIII at 1743 GMT on June 6, 1964. Sailplane made flight from Reno, Nevada. (location indicated by dot on nephanalysis and on Tiros picture.)

Satellite photo of Sierra Wave superimposed on nephanalysis of weather system for June 6, 1944.

distance wave flight on February 5, 1965, releasing in a wave over Minden, Nevada, at 10,000 feet and working his way 250 miles northeast at 24,000 feet to Elko in 5½ hours. Lindsay checked the Tiros pictures for that day and guessed Beebe could have flown considerably farther downwind, had he so desired.

A Tiros V photograph made on April 18, 1963, revealed a strong wave pattern extending more than 100 miles eastward of the Appalachian Mountains, over Virginia, West Virginia, and North Carolina. While ground observers saw "lennies" in eastern Virginia, no waves were reported by pilots in the air at that time, possibly, Lindsay conjectured, because the wave length was 13 miles from crest to crest and the pilots were flying low.

Until satellite pictures of large wave patterns became available, soaring pilots utilized mountain waves primarily for high-altitude rather than long-distance flights. In the lee of the Appalachian chain, wave flights have exceeded 20,000 feet over Vermont and western North Carolina, and have been made to 17,000 feet over western Maryland.

In New Zealand, S.H. Georgeson rode a mountain wave 460 miles out and back from Omarama, near the Southern Alps, for a world record that stood until Karl Stiedieck beat him on March 3, 1968, with a remarkable demonstration of ridge soaring, 476.6 miles on a planned round trip from Eagleville, Pennsylvania, along the Appalachians to Mountain Grove, Virginia, and back. A South African, Bobby Clifford, topped this record by 11.7 miles on New Years Day, 1969.

The intriguing possibility of soaring 1,000 miles and more has been advanced by a meteorologist, John H. Aldrich, supervising aviation forecaster of the Los Angeles Weather Bureau Forecast Center. To accomplish such a feat, he suggested the pilot take the up-elevator in a mountain wave to 35,000 feet, then climb over the core of a jet stream, from its clear south side to the cloudy north side, and settle into a bubble of high-velocity wind, called the *jet max,* which travels as much as 200 mph. Six hours later he would dive out of the jet stream and land, perhaps 1,200 miles from his starting point. Oxygen would, of course, be necessary on such a remarkable flight, and the advent of pressurized gliders will very likely hasten the day when jet-stream soaring becomes a *fait accompli.*

Super Cub with 150-hp engine tows Schweizer 2-33 sailplane into air off Crystalaire Airport, California.

# 8/THE SKY SURFERS

SURFING HAS TAKEN TO THE SERENELY BEAUTIFUL SKIES of Hawaii's Oahu Island—high above the long, curling breakers of Waikiki and Makaha, where soaring pilots enjoy a glorious year-round freedom of motion surpassing even the graceful sweep of a surfboard flashing through white foam. Instead of the thunder of the surf, a soaring pilot hears only the caress of wind over wings, the keening cry of a distant seabird. "This is without doubt the greatest ridge soaring site in the world," says Thomas J. Winkler, Sr., president of the Hawaii Soaring Club, who speaks with the authority of more than 33 years soaring experience in Europe, the U.S.A., and finally the "Islands." In the classic documentary film, *The Endless Summer,* a worldwide search is conducted for the perfect ocean wave for surfing; Winkler similarly searched mountain slopes of the world for the perfect atmospheric surfing site, and found it in Hawaii.

Along the windward side of Oahu stretches a range of mountains called the Waianae, its 4,000-foot slope stretching across northwest trade winds that blow over the island 12 months of the year. So permanent is the "built-in" lift it provides, that there is virtually no limit to the length of time a soaring craft can stay aloft, except the physical endurance of the pilot. For this reason the Federation Aeronautique Internationale removed duration flights from record competition—they serve only to prove that soaring is easy, exciting, and endless.

Here, on the Waianae ridge, man has duplicated and even surpassed dynamic soaring feats of the graceful albatross, sweeping back and forth along a slope where winds turn waterfalls upside down. Here, Winkler set an unofficial world record in August, 1968, soaring solo for 50 hours 16 minutes—300 times longer than Orville Wright's 1911 record flight at Kitty Hawk! And here, in 1961, two other soaring pilots stayed aloft 71 hours 5 minutes—nearly three days and nights—alternately flying and sleeping.

On the Big Island, Hawaii, the mighty volcanos of Mauna Loa and

Mauna Kea thrust up to more than 13,000 feet, generating waves on which Woodson K. Woods of the Mauna Kea Soaring Club reached twice that height, 26,000 feet. When an occasional weather front moves across, a new world altitude record for sailplanes could be made, say boosters of Hawaii's sky surfing.

On February 25, 1961, an amazing altitude flight to more than nine miles was finally made in California's mighty Sierra Wave, an experience that would remain unduplicated for a full decade and promised to continue unchallenged, until someone in a pressurized glider rides the same fantastic wave system. The pilot was Paul Bikle, director of NASA's Flight Research Center at Edwards Air Force Base, the man who planned flights of such rocket ships as the North American X-15. Bikle's love is soaring, the challenge of riding the high sky on the power of Mother Nature herself. His home is in Lancaster, in a lower part of the Mojave Desert called Antelope Valley, a soaring pilot's paradise; the configuration of mountain ranges makes wave flying possible under a wide range of wind conditions. The strongest waves occur to the north, near Bishop, where on the evening of February 24, 1961, meteorologist Harold Klieforth alerted Bikle that a cold front was approaching at a velocity sufficient to generate a good mountain wave.

At nearby Fox Field, Bikle readied his sailplane the next morning; to the northeast appeared the familiar mother-of-pearl lenticular cloud marking the Sierra Wave like a giant signpost. Nearer, transient fragments of wave cloud formed and dissipated, evidence of strong local lift. His sailplane was a Schweizer 1-23E, a mid-wing cantilever ship of metal construction, with thin wings tapering to 51 feet. Its L/D glide ratio was a good 30:1, its minimum sink only two feet per second. Inside the small cockpit, Bikle installed a pressure-demand oxygen system, good to about 45,000 feet.

With barographs in place, Bikle climbed in and signaled his tow pilot. Soon they were climbing northward toward Mojave, where the first pulses of lift appeared, marking a wave east of the Tehachapi Mountains. At about 10,000 feet Bikle cut loose to begin his hunt. He blundered into an area of rapid sink, and pushed the Schweizer's nose down to dive through it as fast as possible, close to the redline speed of 130 mph. This served a double purpose—getting through sink fast conserved altitude, and yet the lower he flew, the better chance he had to establish a record for altitude gain, for physiological limitations put his ceiling at that of his oxygen system.

Paul Bikle, NASA Flight Research Center director, climbed his Schweizer 1-23E sail-plane to a world record altitude of 46,267 feet above sea level in the Sierra Wave on February 25, 1961; he also claimed the record for 42,303-foot altitude gain.

Ahead, in Owens Valley east of the Sierras, blowing dust covered the desert floor; the wind swooped upward almost vertically to form an ominous roll cloud. If he could reach that wind shear, he could regain his lost height, though the ride would be dangerous. For a moment it looked as if he'd have to land; his eyes scanned the ground for a landing site. Suddenly the Schwiezer shuddered. Bikle zoomed the glider into a steep climb, grabbing for altitude.

Further north he slipped on his oxygen mask and adjusted the flow valve, carefully groping his way ahead of the ugly roll cloud as he neared the lenticular. Higher and higher he climbed; at 25,000 feet an icy cold penetrated his heavy altitude clothes. The thermometer read -20° C; frost coated his canopy. At 30,000 feet and -40° C, higher than Mount Everest, he was

129

sealed inside a white cocoon, floating skyward at a steady dreamlike pace, unable to see out. Flying on instruments, he concentrated on a vital decision—to go on climbing or turn back.

Paul Bikle knew from his research at the NASA Flight Test Center the dangers of pushing oneself too far, beyond a point of no return. From personal experience in altitude chambers he had set his own time limit—only ten minutes above 40,000 feet. Further, his oxygen supply would soon be exhausted. He checked his watch as he passed 40,000 feet, with the outside air temperature now down to -60° C. The only sound was the soft sigh of his oxygen valve, the brush of wind. He pressed on.

The Schweizer climbed more slowly, less than 500 feet per minute, the altimeter needle inching agonizingly toward 45,000 feet. Allowing for instrument error, that would insure a world record. With his oxygen supply low and time running out, he finally conceded defeat to the icy emptiness of near space. He might have climbed another mile, but in doing so he also might have died, as did Karl Oevgaard, the first martyr to stratospheric soaring. He swung the nose around and dove downwind, across the lenticular to its trailing edge, into the strong downdrafts.

Schweizer 2-32 sailplane ridge-soars along Sierra Estrellas, near Phoenix, Arizona.

Two hours 10 minutes after takeoff, Bikle completed his amazing flight, settling down through the late afternoon sky to land at Fox. FAI calibration of his barograph confirmed what he already knew—he was the new world's altitude soaring champion! He had climbed to an absolute height of 46,267 feet above sea level, and had set another world record by gaining 42,303 feet above the lowest point of his flight.

Conquest of the high sky in gliders is one thing, but to most soaring pilots the real challenge is cross-country sailplaning, which requires skill, good judgment, much patience, and lots of luck. There is also the unique thrill of drawing upon the energy of the sky itself, working the windward slope of a mountain range, or circling to great heights in a thermal bubble only to slide down in a swift, easy "toboggan" glide in search of the next one. All that must be done is find currents of air rising faster than the sink rate of the sailplane, and so go on coasting mile after mile, following river valleys, mountain systems, warm patches of earth, and even cities, towns, and highways, wherever the elemental heat of the sun is converted into rising air by convectivity.

International glider distance records held by United States pilots were few and far between in the postwar years, but on July 15, 1947, Paul Mac-Cready flew a glider to a new goal-and-return record of 230 miles, from Wichita Falls to Buzz Field, near Roaring Springs, Texas, in a craft nicknamed the *Screamin' Weiner,* for the shrill whine it made while climbing on tow. A short span sailplane with high wing loading, it was developed before the war, but MacCready loved it; he claimed it could outperform a hawk if flown properly.

Efforts were made in 1947 to stimulate interest in soaring among the youth of America; Nevada Senator Pat McCarran introduced in Congress a bill to establish a Youth Training Division of the Civil Aeronautics Administration, to augment a National Glider Training Program, and the Soaring Society of America followed by recommending that the National Park Service develop soaring sites similar to that at Big Meadows in Shenandoah National Park. Neither proposal succeeded, and moreover better ships were needed before any postwar surge of interest could take place.

131

Soaring gets to people of all ages. Here, Mark Firkins, a teenage student pilot gets set for his first lesson in the cockpit of a Schweizer 2-33.

Soaring in America came of age when a search got under way to find a glider type better suited to long-distance flight than surplus trainers left over from World War II. Ben Shupack, secretary of the Soaring Society of America, instituted a series of conferences on motorless flight to exchange ideas among progressive sailplane enthusiasts, and at a meeting of the SSA and the Institute of Aeronautical Sciences in 1948, the basic design concept for a record-breaking sailplane was developed.

In that year, a student at Mississippi State University, Richard H. Johnson, contracted with sailplane designer, Harland Ross, to build such a soaring craft; in January, 1950, after Ross had completed 60 percent of the airframe, Johnson took the craft to MSU to see what refinements he and the late aerodynamicist, Dr. August Raspet, could incorporate. "The design was somewhat modified," Johnson recalled, "principally in raising the wing location from mid to high position, to improve its aerodynamic efficiency. The ship was completed and first flown the following June, when flight test measurements showed an L/D of about 33:1. Modifications made that

Dick Johnson's RJ-5 sailplane, the first specially designed after World War II to go after distance records.

winter—an improved canopy and removal of the 'spoilerons'—increased the L/D to about 38.5:1; and finally, the use of flush skin raised that to about 40:1 in 1952."

With this remarkable craft, Johnson set out to beat the world distance record of 749 kilometers (465 miles) set in 1939 by the Russian girl pilot, Olga Klepikova. On August 8, 1951, he left Odessa, Texas, in the RJ-5 (named for Ross and Johnson), to cloud hop north under a sky cottony with cumulus puffs, each marking the top of a rising thermal bubble. So well did pilot and sailplane perform that in nearly nine hours he worked his way far north across the great central plains country, using the lifting power of 37 separate thermals, stretching 80-mph glides from the top of one to the bottom of the next, and finally came down at Salina, Kansas, 535 miles distant. In covering 861 kilometers, Johnson raised the possibility that soon the goal of 1,000 kilometers could be reached and surpassed. He'd simply run out of daylight, for when he landed, at 7:15 P.M., Kansas lay cool under an evening sky and thermaling was finished for the day.

Paul Bikle held no thought of setting a distance record when he set off at high noon on July 24, 1963, from Sun Valley, Idaho, in a Prue Standard sailplane, after an airplane tow to 7,500 feet from the mile-high airport. He began working his way north along the Continental Divide, west of a frontal storm system. He hadn't bothered to bring a barograph—after all, he held all the FAI badges there were to hold. It was a rough but exciting trip, through turbulence and vicious downdrafts that tested his nerve and coordination. A lesser pilot might have turned back, but Bikle pushed on, crossing the Salmon River, and there ran out of the scattered cumulus clouds that were his "stepping stones" across the Rockies. Ahead lay a massive thunderstorm; Bikle headed for it. Strong winds sucked him up to the cloud base at 16,500 feet, through pelting hail. He drove ahead, found a new storm and went for that. Great Falls, Montana, slipped by, and in the flat valley of the Missouri River he looked down on a grand spectacle of elemental fury, with dust storms and mountainous cloud formations marking the advance of the giant storm system. Out of oxygen, he flew lower, at 15,000 feet, and crossed the wide Missouri. Ahead lay the opportunity to exceed the world record of Dick Johnson, though it would be unofficial. He raced on toward the north, diving through fantastic updrafts at 100 mph to stay ahead of the lightning-laced storm that seemed ready to swallow him. He'd flown beyond the limits of his maps; he could only guess how far he had penetrated inside Canada when darkness came. Finally he called it a day, and landed in a plowed field near Swift Current, Saskatchewan, 557 miles from Sun Valley, almost 900 kilometers.

The first soaring pilot to break the 1,000-kilometer "barrier" in a sailplane was Alvin H. Parker, an Odessa financier, flying a sleek Sisu 1A, a craft strong enough for acrobatic flight and clean enough to glide at an L/D of 44:1, and to regain, in a single climbing turn, altitude lost diving between thermals 20 miles apart at 120 miles an hour. Seeking a record goal flight of 1,013 kilometers, Parker set off from Odessa on the morning of July 24, 1964, and headed north over the Great Plains, riding the early thermals. As they built up under the warming sun, he watched the puffy cumulus grow into thunderheads, which finally forced him to abandon his goal flight. He continued on to Kimball, Nebraska, landing 1,036 kilometers (633 miles) from Odessa. One week later, Parker repeated the performance with his elegant Sisu 1A, soaring 647.17 miles northward to set an official

134

Two old timers—Gus Briegleb, American soaring expert, shows formation problem with hands to Wolfgang Klemperer, builder of the world's first streamlined sailplane, the *Blue Mouse,* at El Mirage Airport, California.

world distance record. On August 8, 1969, he also established a world goal flight record of 570 miles (917 kilometers). Releasing from an airplane tow to 3,200 feet above Odessa Airport, he worked his way to Blanding, Utah, crossing over the field at 1,000 feet, 9 hours 53 minutes later. On this flight, Parker exceeded by 50 miles an earlier goal record of 520.5 miles set by Wallace Scott in 1964, who in turn had beaten a still earlier record of Parker's. On August 22, 1969, Scott came back to defeat Parker once more with a splendid goal flight from Odessa to Gila Bend, Arizona, 606.24 miles distant. Scott used a graceful new ASW 12, designed by Alexander Schliecher, a Wasserkuppe pilot-designer of world fame. The craft had a maximum glide ratio of 48:1 at 62 miles an hour, and a featherlight sink of only 1.6 feet per second at 46 miles an hour.

Such are the design improvements in sailplanes since 1948 that a whole new world of flight has opened, one in which the gentlest zephyr may be sufficient to keep a modern soaring craft afloat. No longer are the strong slope winds of the Wasserkuppe, or the mighty chimney drafts of the Sierra Wave, essential to record soaring flights. In distant parts of the world, today's sky surfers find lift as handily as a hawk, if not for record setting, at least

135

for a satisfying an hour or two of cross-country thermaling.

A popular soaring site is the broad plateau at Baragawnath, in South Africa, where massive cumulus clouds build up daily over the Rand. Here, two world records fell in a single day, December 28, 1967, summertime south of the equator. Maurice "Bomber" Jackson set a 500-kilometer tri-angular course speed record of 84.08 mph in a South African sailplane, the BJ3, while Yvonne Leeman, in a Phoebus, ranged out and back 385.66 miles for a feminine record. Here too, in 1951, a Swiss engineer, Rene Comte, flew his Mowsey (buzzard) IV sailplane into a giant thunderhead and had a wild ride through pelting hail and violent turbulence to 32,000 feet, higher than anyone had flown in a glider over Africa. Dazzling light-ning exploded around him, Comte reported. "The whole cloud lit up, with me inside it. I felt lightning hit the top of my head a sharp blow and run through my hands into the control column. The plane continued to fly steady, but I was scared."

Arizona emerged as a favorite postwar western soaring site when modern sailplanes began probing wave patterns created by steady westerly winds blowing over that state's picturesque mountain ranges. Actually, the first soaring in Arizona was done in 1939, when Peter Riedel of Germany crossed the Continental Divide from Winslow to Magdelena, New Mexico in a two-place Karnish. Riedel found it necessary to soar at 18,000 feet, where each breath delivers to the lungs only half the amount of oxygen available at sea level. Fearing anoxia, he shouted loudly to himself to stay

Line boy prepares to attach tow rope; Crystalaire.

conscious, "using some strong expressions to pep myself up," he said later. "I even tried to sing, but found that it was not at all advisable, because one had to breath often and deeply at such altitudes." Joseph C. Lincoln, who learned to soar at Falcon Field, near Mesa, in 1956, became the first Arizonan to earn the coveted Diamond C, which requires a distance flight of 500 kilometers, a 300-mile goal flight, and an altitude gain of 5,000 kilometers. In 1960 Lincoln won the Barringer Trophy by soaring 455.5 miles from Prescott to Variadero, New Mexico. In 1970, the Arizona Soaring Association numbered 40 members, and throughout the state were a total of 30 private and club gliders. ARA member Bill Ordway reported that "tremendous waves have been observed off the San Francisco Peaks near Flagstaff, but have never been contacted. We estimate that flights to 40,000 feet are possible in the primary wave there." In addition, Ordway reported good ridge soaring along the Sierra Estrella range southwest of Phoenix, and excellent spring and summer thermals over the low desert and high plateau regions of the state. In 1969, Ordway and two other pilots soared from Prescott to Albuquerque, 326 miles, and the next spring, a time when upper west winds are strongest, began shooting for record-breaking goal-and-return flights of 400 to 500 miles.

There are things to be learned about soaring in Arizona, things that can mean the difference between a championship flight and disaster. Veteran glider pilot Fred Robinson, operator of the Great Western Soaring School at Crystalaire Country Club Airport, on the Mojave Desert of southern California, learned at first hand the dangers of venturing too close to turgid squall lines that sometimes build over the Coconino Plateau, north of the Mogollon Rim. Here, in true Zane Grey country, aerial riders of the purple haze confront brutal elemental forces that would make a western gunslinger run for cover. Early one July morning in 1966, Robinson rolled out his Schweizer 1-26 homebuilt at Crystalaire, eyed a line of cumulus puffballs drifting eastward at 14,000 feet, and figured this was the day to go for his Diamond C distance of 310 miles. For the first four hours the cross country flight was uneventful; he flew from thermal to thermal, working his way east to the Colorado River, his first check point. Ahead lay a long cloud street, marking an upper low-pressure through with considerable instability.

"Then I spotted another cloud street to the south, about fifteen miles distant," Robinson related, as he and I sat in his trailer office at Crystalaire,

Tradition—you lose your shirt tail when you solo, as author found out.

discussing the flight. It was there that Robinson, in 1969, signed off my own private glider license, and introduced me to the world of sailplaning and to the wonderful people who come from over the world to enjoy this paradise of soaring above the lower Mojave.

In the late afternoon, Robinson continued, the cumulus began to over-build. A warning bell rang in his head, but he disregarded it—he could make out the runway of Grand Canyon Airport in the distance, 320 miles from home, just right for a Diamond flight. "I was so elated I began to sing; I would be the first United States pilot to earn his Diamond Badge in a 1-26. I was at 13,000 feet, and began a straight glide for the airport."

Perhaps he was too busy counting his blessings, Robinson said, for only then did he realize with a shock that the two cloud streets had merged into a V, with his sailplane in the middle. "I was in blue sky, but to north and south of me were lines of heavy thunderstorms with much precipitation. Within minutes the two storm systems converged into one."

Suddenly he was flying through drenching sheets of rain that obliterated the ground from view. There was nothing to do but turn and run for it, abandoning all thought of reaching the Grand Canyon. "My single goal was survival now, to find a place to land, but at 13,000 feet, flying along the edge of the exploding storm cloud, I was running into heavy headwinds that reduced my ground speed to near zero. I finally spotted a field in the dusk and opened my dive brakes, circling in an area of sink. At 2,000 feet

138

I saw that the field was an orchard with trees pruned back, so I hurried back into the lift area and climbed once more to the cloud base at 13,000."

In the semi-darkness, Robinson searched for another landing field he knew to be in the area, at Dobb's Ferry; it was obscured in blinding rain. Alarmed now, he glanced south, and made out the dim contour of an alkali flat called Red Lake. He lowered the glider's nose to pick up speed, and at 90 mph was barely moving over the ground. To his amazement, a black, inverted funnel formed over the lakebed, and became a whirling tornado! He hurried away, found a long ridge extending outward from an extinct volcano and there gained enough altitude to once more head for Kingman, back toward the Colorado River. In the distance he finally saw the rotating beacon light of Kingman Airport, but headway was virtually impossible in the turbulent windstorm generated by the giant cumulonimbus overhead. The early night was black; in the east a full moon rose to give an eerie glow to the scene. Reading his flight instruments by the light of frequent lightning flashes, he began a long shallow dive for Kingman, when wisps of cloud appeared over his left wing. He was being sucked inside the cloud itself! Robinson prepared to bail out, then remembered the fate of three German pilots trapped inside such a storm; two parachuted down frozen to death; the third was charred by lightning.

"My wings were still on," he recalled, "so I pulled on the dive brakes and shoved the stick forward, banging my head on the canopy. The nose was almost straight down, and my airspeed was up to 100 mph before I stopped

Sleek Diamant sailplane is designed with small frontal area, with pilot lying supine under plexiglass bubble.

climbing. In a few moments I came out through the bottom, amidst more flashes of lightning. I ran through some hail that hammered violently against the canopy, but I was determined to reach Kingman, and my only worry now was running into another ship in the dark, for I had no lights. I finally reached the field and set the ship down on the runway, to bring to an end quite an exciting ten-hour flight." When he stepped out, Robinson laughed, "I fell smack on my face; my legs were numb!" Since that day, Robinson has won his coveted Diamond Badge with a 335-mile flight in an HP-11A, and has exceed 300 miles 11 times, once soaring 370 miles into northeast Arizona.

The soaring pilot's sky is crowded with adventure and excitement for those who seek it on record attempts, but for the majority of the 10,000 and more glider enthusiasts in America, soaring is one of the safest and most enjoyable of sports. Much of the enjoyment is in coping with local weather patterns, which produce lift in a variety of ways.

On a recent spring day the author took an airliner to San Jose, California, with the expectation of enjoying a day's sailplaning at nearby Sky Sailing Airport, a favorite soaring site close to rolling green foothills below 2,508-foot Mission Peak, a rocky upthrusting where flocks of goats and golden eagles offer companionship to lonely riders of the wind. Not far distant is Mount Hamilton, the site of John J. Montgomery's later gliding experiments.

Low clouds and rain squalls greeted me at San Jose, marking the passage of a fast-moving frontal system with winds gusting to 40 knots. Rather than dampen spirits, it promised good soaring weather the following day, when a post-frontal cold air mass and gentler winds could produce a combination of thermal and ridge lift. And sure enough, it was a day to be long remembered! Traditionally, glider pilots shake their heads and say, "You should have been here yesterday!" But on this occasion I saw wide grins and flashing eyes as pilots returned from the ridge.

Hetty Treese invited me to check out in a Schweizer 2-33 and learn the secrets of Mission Ridge, known to those who have spent long hours soaring there. Soon we were in tow behind a Super Cub, climbing under the base of fresh, building cumulus clouds drifting across San Francisco Bay and historic Fremont out of the northwest, directly across the slope.

"Down there," Hetty pointed. "See that big tree on the ridge? Don't let the wind drift you back of that, or you'll find dangerous sink in the valley behind it. We lost a glider there last year."

140

We'd released at 1,900 feet and already were climbing past 2,500 feet, higher than the peak itself, as we crabbed along the ridge.

"Open the spoilers," Hetty suggested. "Let's go back down and ride the elevator again! I want to show you something."

We turned away from the ridge in the first half of a figure eight pattern by which we remained in good lift, and then once more slewed along the rocky terrain, the tip of our slender wing seeming to scrape the foliage. Behind me, Hetty laughed excitedly. "Look! With full spoilers we're still climbing 700 feet a minute!"

Once we'd learned where the best low ridge lift was, and where down-drafts lurked, we headed for the high ridge to spend an exhilarating hour, playing tag with a gorgeous golden eagle and looking across to white-mantled Mount Hamilton. What Montgomery wouldn't have given to enjoy such a day of soaring more than half a century ago!

Schweizer 2-32 in tow behind Holiday school tugplane, at Tehachapi.

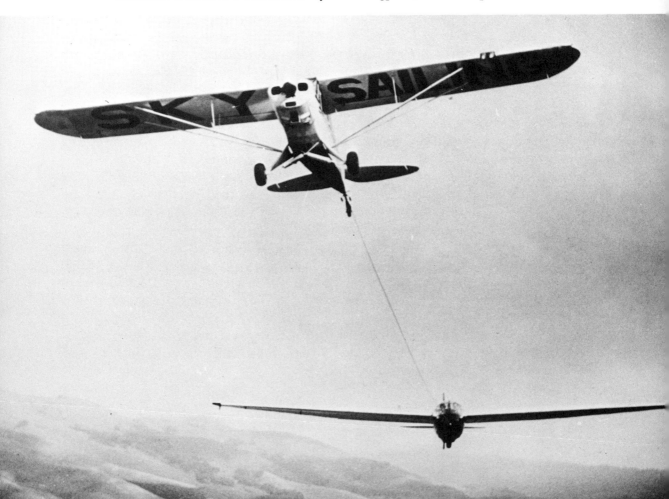

Well known to southern California soaring pilots is the classic "smog front," which exists along a wind shear line marking the advance of a polluted marine air convergence from the Los Angeles Basin, as it blows inland during the afternoons, spilling around the Santa Ana Mountains into the Elsinore area, and through Mint Canyon and Cajon Pass onto the Mojave Desert. Along this shear line are located some of the west's finest soaring schools—at Elsinore, at Tehachapi, at Crystalaire, and at El Mirage, the latter a dry lake bed which served as a wartime pilot training base. The smog front is easy to see, and rather than run from the smelly, choking Los Angeles air, glider pilots run toward it, for as the cool coastal air slides in under the warmer desert air, solid lift occurs.

Over El Mirage, whirling dust devils appear whenever the smog front approaches. On July 30, 1964, two expert sailplaners, Hannes Linke and William Ivans, stood watching them. It was a perfect day to try for a 100-kilometer speed run, south to Wrightwood, west over Crystalaire to Littlerock, and thence back to El Mirage, utilizing both the Cajon Pass and Mint Canyon shear lines. The first time around, Linke missed the turning point at Wrightwood, while Ivans finished the course at 83.786 mph in his Sisu 1A. Linke tried again, heading his Libelle between two giant dust devils toward the smog front. "I flew along the shear line and came out at the end of the cloud street at 11,500 feet, four miles out from the Wrightwood turn-point," he related. "Then I headed northwest toward Crystalaire. A little east of the strip was a nice cloud street; I just went underneath the edge and thermaled from 7,500 up to 9,500. When it weakened I headed for Littlerock, and there hit fairly strong sink. I decided I'd better pick up something on the way home, and made one unnecessary circle in weak lift. Things picked up after that, and I had just enough altitude left to run it home at 115 knots, and cross the finish line at 100 feet." Linke's time of 44 minutes 24 seconds gave him a slight edge over Ivans, with a speed average of 84.9 mph, but not enough to claim a new record if Ivans put in for one. A true sportsman, Ivans withdrew his claim, allowing Linke to become the new world record holder as a German national, while Ivans claimed the U.S. national record for the 100-kilometer course.

For all his expertise, Hannes Linke admitted to being tricked by a rotor cloud at the 1968 Reno Nationals: "I was on oxygen at 22,000 feet, high above the Sierras, in air that was serenely smooth. Paul Bikle came sliding under me, only ten feet below. We waved at each other. After a while I headed back to the field, at Stead Air Force Base, confident there'd be the usual thermals to get me over the intervening ridge. Instead I ran into unexplained sink; I sadly spiraled down into the valley to land. There I caught a small thermal, over a little knoll, and worked it back high enough to top the ridge. I felt lucky to make the field, until I heard another pilot radio down from the stratosphere—there was a dry wave blowing; I'd been booby-trapped by a rotor I couldn't see!"

Bill Ivans remembered running into a dry thermal in his Sisu 1A on a goal flight from Minden, Nevada, to Susanville, California, and return, during the 1965 Western Regional Soaring Championships, in which he averaged 51.5 mph to win the event over the 211-mile course: "At Frenchman Reservoir, 70 miles out," he related, "the clouds stop. Susanville is 35 miles away, and the sky over the lowlands appears ominously devoid of both thermal activity and gliders. We manage to reach 12,500 feet under the last cloud, and set out at best gliding speed along the edge of Honey Lake, staying over the high ground.

"The roller coaster ride of the past 60 miles now becomes a nervous watching for signs of thermal activity and a calculation of glide distance in still air. Instead of 130 mph, we now fly at a sedate 65; the altitude in hand may have to take us a long way, and we have a much flatter glide at the lower airspeed.

"A dry thermal alongside Honey Lake is circled in with loving care, and rewards us with 13,000 feet only 25 miles from Susanville, which is at an elevation of 4,150 feet. We can now glide to the goal with ease, but by no means are we sure of a return of our thermal generating air mass.

"Then, incredibly, a single cloud begins to form over the single small mountain in the flat marsh area between Honey Lake and the goal. It is the only cloud within 20 miles of Susanville!" Without that cloud Ivans' flight would have ended, but it gave him just enough extra lift to continue his tortuous flight to goal and back.

The first woman in the United States to win her Diamond Badge was Helen Dick, a documentation officer with the U.S. Coast Guard in San Diego, who in 1956, she says, became "hooked" on gliding in a TG-2 flight at Elsinore. "It was absolutely beautiful!" she recalled. "The wind was from the east and the big ridge was booming with ridge lift. The mountains were snow covered—we could see the ocean and the sun was just beginning to turn the snow beautiful reds."

On July 12, 1964, Helen made her Diamond Goal flight from Inyokern, east of the Sierras, to Laws, a small town to the north near Bishop, and

Author poses beside Schweizer 2-32 which he flew from Holiday school at Tehachapi in preparation for this book.

back to Inyokern, in a Zugvogel IIIB sailplane she partly owned. No wave was blowing, though a cloud street extended down the length of the Sierra range. The flight took 6 hours 49 minutes and was recorded as 248.82 miles, earning her the U.S. National Goal and Return record. Her altitude gain flight for the Diamond was made at Tehachapi on May 30, 1967, a gain of more than 17,000 feet. "It was one of the most beautiful I've had," she remembered, "because of the view of the desert from that altitude, also the mountains and coastal areas." Her most satisfying flight was the Diamond distance flight itself, on August 12, 1967, when she left El Mirage for Laws, working a cloud street that formed ahead of her over the White Mountains to the east of Owens Valley. "I was able to go along the top of the Whites without circling; I would merely drive ahead in the areas of down and slow up when encountering lift areas, and thus was able to fly almost 50 miles in a straight line." After four hours of soaring, Helen arrived at her turn-point 200 miles north of El Mirage, flew over the valley to take pictures proving she'd been there, and headed for the hills once more, following a cloud street leading to Tonopah, Nevada. It was late afternoon and thermal lift was diminishing. Helen was losing altitude fast, and down to 1,500 feet above the ground she spotted an orange windsock on a small landing strip at Millett, Nevada. She landed, much to the surprise of local ranchers, who took her to a telephone to call her ground crew. She'd covered a total

144

of 324 miles, including 305.84 in a straight line for the U.S. national distance record for women.

A controversy exists today among sky surfers, as to the propriety of adding an engine to a glider. Purists say it spoils the essential beauty and challenge of soaring flight, while advocates claim you can soar just as well with the engine off, and besides, it provides you with extra independence in launch and gives you a way to get home when the thermals stop. Back in 1923, a Frenchman named Georges Bardot crossed the English Channel and returned in 1 hour 45 minutes, by climbing in a powered glider to 5,000 feet, shutting down the engine and soaring over. In that same year, a German pilot, Franz Budig, former chief constructor for the Rumpler works, built a powered glider with a two-cylinder motorcycle engine of four-hp equipped for aerial restart. Numerous other powered gliders have since appeared, and while detractors say such compromise makes them neither a good airplane nor a good sailplane, there is much to be said in their favor in introducing power pilots to the art of soaring. The author was invited to fly such a craft, the Fournier RF4D, a metal low-wing ship with a 40-hp Volkswagen-Rectimo engine. It performed well on a flight from Fox Field, near Lancaster, California; at 5,000 feet the engine was shut down and a climb of 250 feet per minute established in a weak wave. A similar craft, the RW-3, is powered with a Porsche engine, has retractable tricycle landing gear and a propeller in back. One of the best perform-

The propeller of an RW-3 stopped in streamline position.

Latest of popular new "motorsailers" (powered gliders) is the ASK 14 Motorsegler, with 29-hp engine shown stopped. Pilots use power for takeoff, shut down to soar, then fly home on power.

ing powered gliders is the highly streamlined ASK 14 Motorsegler, designed by Alexander Schleicher, which offers excellent soaring capabilities with a 29-hp engine, enabling it to take off from any sailplane base with ease. According to its designer, "as a rule, the engine is used very sparingly. Take-offs, including the initial hunting for lift, very rarely take more than three to five minutes." The ASK 14's glide ratio is 29:1.

Just as gliders went to war in the 1940's, so today, powered gliders are again taking their place in the military inventory. LTV Electrosystems, of Greenville, Texas produced the L450F, a turboprop unmanned drone for electronic reconnaissance flights, a design derived from the Schweizer SGS 2-32 sailplane; Lockheed similarly produced a "quiet airplane" derivation of the 2-32, designated the YO-3A. A third powered glider, claiming a higher L/D performance than either of the military craft, is Jim Bede's B-2, in which he hoped to circle the world nonstop in 1970.

There have been other "freak" motorsailers in the past and there'll be more in the future; although soaring on the power of the wind is one thing and flying a gas buggy another. Light plane pilots frequently throttle back while flying through atmospheric waves, wind shears, and thermals, to conserve fuel, and most soaring pilots will claim their feel for thermals gives them greater skill at flying powered craft. At El Mirage, Gus Briegleb, a veteran glider pilot who once trained an eagle to sniff out thermals for him, is an expert at riding dust devils in a Piper Cub with the engine off.

In the decade of the 1970's, great advances are sure to be made in soaring, through new designs, new materials, new construction techniques; one

146

proposal calls for a giant sailplane with a span of 100 feet and an aspect ratio of 30:1, which promises an L/D glide ratio of better than 47:1. By soaring in the jet stream, distances in excess of 1,000 miles are possible, in pressurized sailplanes. A high-aspect-ratio, all-wing sailplane design may become the super-soarer of tomorrow, and designs are being considered for variable-geometry (moveable wing) gliders built expressly for speed record flying.

Sorely needed is a practical thermal detector, with a useful range and a cost low enough for the average weekend soaring pilot; one such concept already is now under study. Early in 1970, Major General C.F. Von Kahn, a vice president of the Air Transport Association of America, warned that "we need to mount an attack on clear air turbulence to be able to see it, avoid it, or adjust our penetrations." Such an attack already has been mounted, by Commander George Michanowsky of New York, in an effort to help the aviation industry meet the danger of clear air turbulence (CAT) in triple-sonic SST flights. During explorations of the Andes in South America, Commander Michanowsky was inspired by the performance of soaring condors, to wonder whether some particular spectral wavelength was used by them to see CAT. In making aerial reconnaissances of archeological sites in that region, he was able to pick up ultraviolet "signatures" of atmospheric perturbations. According to film experts at the Eastman Kodak Company, Michanowsky is breaking new ground with his ideas on near-ultraviolet CAT detection, the success of which could make visible to soaring pilots for the first time, the whole wonderful world of ever-changing currents in the sky.

Ryan Aeronautical Company is experimenting with "Rogollo" wings for glider transportation of freight, tanks, etc.

# INDEX

## A

Abaris, 1
Airborne Transport, Inc., 81
Alison, Col. John R., 105
Archytas, 1
Arnold, Maj. Gen. H. H., 70, 72
Asia, gliders in, 104 ff.

## B

Bardot, Georges, 145
Barnaby, Ralph S., 59, 62
Barringer, Lewin B., 63–67, 72; ill., 73
Beebe, Bruce, 123
Bell, Dr. Alexander, 24, 28
Bikle, Paul, 128–131, 134, 142; ill., 129
Bladud, King, 1
Blume, Walter, 36
Bowlus, Fred, 84
Bowlus, Hawley, 54–58, 84; ill., 55, 57
Bowlus Sailplane Co., 62
Boyle, Capt. Jacque, 102
Brauer, Karl, 41; ill., 42
Briegleb, Gus, 146; ill., 135
Brown, Woodbridge P., 57, 63
Budig, Franz, 145

## C

Cayley, Sir George, 6; ill., 7
Chanute, Octave, 5, 11, 22, 27, 28; ill., 16
Colditz Cock, 98
Comte, Rene, 136
Crete glider attack, 88
Criz, Albert, 81, 83
Curtiss, Glenn, 24–25, 53, 71

## D

Daedalus, and Icarus, 1
Darwin, Charles, 2
Da Vinci, Leonardo, 4
D-Day glider invasion, 99 ff.
Decker, Chester, 79
Dent, Col. Fred R., Jr., 73 ff.
Dick, Helen, 143
Dreschel, Capt. Walter, 50
du Pont, Felix A., 63, 73, 81, 83
du Pont, Richard H., 57–63, 65, 73, 82, 106

## E

Eaton, Warren, 57, 62
Eban, Emael Fortress, 69, 88
Edgar, Larry, 114 ff.; ill., 117, 118
Espenlaub, Gottlieb, 59
Evans, Col. Edward E., 59

## F

Fischer, Berthold, 33
Foehnwall, 120 ff.
Frankfort Sailplane Co., 62
Franklin, Prof. R. E., 59
Fustian Mission, 93

## G

Garrison, Lt. Col. Phil W., 107 ff.
Gliders and Sailplanes
  Advanced trainer, German, ill., 50
  Aerodrome No. 1, 24
  Aeronca TG-5, ill., 73, 75
  Akron Condor, 59
  Austria, 46
  Bat, 17
  Beetle, 17
  BJ-3, 136
  Black Devil, 34–35
  Blue Mouse, 35; ill., 57
  Bowlus Baby Albatross, 55; ill., 56
  Bowlus Falcon, 55
  Bowlus MC-1, 81, 83
  Bowlus No. 16, 55
  Bowlus Senior Albatross, 57
  Bowlus Super Albatross, 57
  Brauer G-1 Albatros, ill., 42
  Brauer SG-2 Etta, 41
  Curtiss June Bug, 25
  Cygnet I, 24
  Daimant, ill., 139
  Darmstadt Konsul, 39, 59
  Douglas XCG-17, ill., 80
  Ente, 38
  Frankfort XTG-1, 74
  Franklin Eaglet, 60; ill., 61
  Franklin utility glider, 59
  FS-3, 39
  Gull, 17
  Halifax, 87
  Hamilcar, 76
  Hawk, 17
  Horsa, 76, 87; ill., 102
  Laister Yankee Doodle, 78
  Laister-Kauffman XCG-10A, ill., 77; 78
  Libelle, 142
  Lore, 42
  Minimoa, ill., 46; 47, 63
  Montgomery Evergreen, 29
  Montgomery Santa Clara, ill., 24
  Moscovitch, 41
  Mowsley IV, 136
  Musterle, 59
  Old Gray Mare, ill., 30; 31
  Parbolic wing glider, 41
  Phoebus, 136
  Piper TG-8, 75
  Powered gliders
    RF4D, 145
    RW-3, 145
    ASK-14, 146
    L-450-F, 146
    YO-3A, 146
    B-2, 146
  Pratt-Read, 116
  Primary trainer, German, ill., 34, 40
  Primary trainer, U.S., ill., 54
  Professor, 39
  Prue Standard, 134
  Rhonadler, 44
  Rhonsperber, 95
  RJ-5, ill., 133
  Rot-Front 7, 48
  Ryan Rogollo wing, ill., 147
  Schleicher ASW-12, 135
  Schweizer 1-23E, 128
  Schweizer 1-26, 137
  Schweizer 1-34, ill., 52
  Schweizer 2-25, 116
  Schweizer 2-32, ill., 66

148

130, 141
Schweizer 2-33, 140; *ill.,*
126, 132
Schweizer SGP 1-1, 62
Schweizer SGU 1-2, 62
Schweizer SGU 1-3, 62
Schweizer TG-3A, 62, 74
Schweizer XTG-2, 74
Schweizer XTG-3, 74
*Screamin' Weiner,* 131
Sisu 1A, 134, 142, 143
Super Sperber, 63
Taylorcraft TG-6, 75
Timm XAG-2, 84
*Vampyr,* 36–40; *ill.,* 38
Waco CG-4A *Flying Jeep,*
72, 75, 78–79, 85,
92 ff.; *ill.,* 88, 103–
104
Waco XCG-13, 76
Wein, 44, 46
XCG-16, 83, 84; *ill.,* 58,
82
XPG-1, -2, -3, 85
Zanonia, 57
Zugvogel IIIB, 144
Gutermuth, Hans, 33

**H**

Harth, Frederic, 33, 37
Hastings, Al, 61
Hawks, Frank, 60–61; *ill.,*
60
Hentzen, Friedrich H., 36,
39
Hesselbach, Peter, 59
Hirth, Wolf, 42, 47, 59
Hoekstra, Harold, 74

**I**

Ivans, William S. Jr., 115,
142–43

**J**

Jackson, Maurice (Bomb-
er), 136
Johnson, Richard H., 132

**K**

Kegel, Max, 43
Kleiforth, Harold, 115
Klemperer, Wolfgang B.,
33–38, 59; *ill.,* 135

Klepikova, Olga, 48, 133;
*ill.,* 49
Koller, Karl, 36
Kraft, Erwin, 48
Kronfeld, Robert, 43–47,
101–102; *ill.,* 45
Kuettner, Dr. A. J., 116

**L**

*Ladbroke Mission,* 92–93;
*ill.,* 86, 90–91
Laister, Jack, 78, 80
Lancaster, Israel, 2
Langley, Professor Samuel,
2, 17
Le Bris, Jean Marie, 5; *ill.,*
6
Leeman, Yvonne, 136
Leusch, Wilhelm, 38
Lilienthal, Otto, 12–17, 23,
28; *ill.,* opp. 1, 14–
15
Lincoln, Joseph C., 137
Lindbergh, Anne, 54; *ill.,*
55
Lindbergh, Charles H., 54;
*ill.,* 55, 57
Linke, Hannes, 120 ff.; 142

**M**

MacCready, Paul, 131
Madelung, Georg, 36
Maloney, Daniel, 27; *ill.,*
26, 28
Maneyrol, Alexis, 39–40
Mantz, Paul, *ill.,* 24
Martens, Arthur, 36, 39
Martin, William H., 30–31
Maxim, Sir Hiram, 1, 5, 17
Michanowsky, Cdr. George,
147
*Moazagotl,* 119
Montgomery, Gen. Bernard,
89
Montgomery, John J., 25–
29, 140; *ill.,* 18, 28
Mouillard, Louis Pierre, 9,
11
Murphy, Lt. Col. M. C.
(Mike), 99–100
Murrell, Melville M., 7; *ill.,*
8
Mussolini, Benito, 94

**N**

Nehring, Johannes, 39, 42,
44

**O**

Oevgaard, Karl Erik, 112,
130
Oliver of Malmsbury, 2
O'Meara, Jack, 59–60
Ordway, William, 137
Ornithopter, 1

**P**

Parker, Alvin H., 134
Parmalee, Phil, 53
Pawlowski, F. W., 69
Pilcher, Percy Sinclair, 16–
17, 28
Proell, Dr. Arthur, 36

**R**

Raspet, Dr. August, 132
Record flights (duration),
25, 36, 37, 39–40,
41, 58, 127
Record flights (distance),
43, 45, 47, 48, 125,
133, 134, 136, 137,
143–145
Record flights (altitude),
39, 50, 65, 131
*Reichenberg Project,* 96 ff.
Reidel, Peter, 48, 63, 136
Reitsch, Hannah, 95 ff.; *ill.,*
96, 98
Ridgeway, Major Matthew B.
89
Robertson Aircraft Co., 79
Robinson, Fred, 137, 140
Robinson, John, 57, 63
Ross, Harland, 111 ff.; *ill.,*
114, 132

**S**

Selfridge, Lt. Thomas, 24
Schultz, Ferdinand, 39
Schweizer Soaring School,
*ill.,* 61–62
Schweizer Aircraft Corp., 62
Shun, Chinese Emperor, 1
Shupack, Ben, 133
Sicily glider invasion, 87 ff.

*Sierra Wave Project,* 111 ff., 128 ff.; *ill.,* 110
Simon the Magician, 1
Skorzeny, Otto, 94–95
Soaring Sites
  Arvin, Calif., 57
  Baragawnath, South Africa, 136
  Cape Cod, Mass., 41, 59
  Crystalaire (Pearblossom, Calif.), 137, 142; *ill.,* 126, 136
  Elmira, N.Y., 57, 59, 63, 65; *ill.,* 61
  El Mirage, Calif., 142, 144, 146
  Elsinore, Calif., 142
  Harris Hill, N.Y., 70; *ill.,* 64
  Itford, England, 39–40
  Minden, Nevada, 143
  Mojave Desert, 57
  New Zealand, 119
  Odessa, Texas, 133–134
  Owens Valley, 71, 111 ff.
  Point Loma, Calif., 58
  Rossiten, Germany, 39
  Russia, 41, 48
  Sky Sailing Airport, Calif. 140
  Sun Valley, Idaho, 134
  Tehachapi, Calif., 141–144
  Torrey Pines, Calif., 56
  Vauville, France, 41
  Wasserkuppe Mt., Germany, 33 ff.; *ill.,* 32, 43

Soaring Societies
  Aachen Aeronautical Society, 34
  Aerial Experiment Association, 24–25
  Aero Club of America, 16, 25
  Aeronautic Society, 25
  Arizona Soaring Association, 137
  Hanover Institute of Technology, 36
  Hawaii Soaring Club, 127
  Mauna Loa Soaring Club, 128
  Mohawk Aerial Navigation & Exploration Co., 12–13
  National Aeronautic Association, 53
  National Glider Association, 59, 62, 69
  Rhon Rossiten Gesellschaft (RRG) Research Institute, 39
  Soaring Society of America, 62, 121–132
  Southern California Soaring Association, 111
Soaring techniques
  Contour cross-country flying, 42
  Dynamic soaring, 39
  Goal flying, 48
  Pickup technique, 107 ff.
  Ridge soaring, 39, 137
  Scientific soaring, 48
  Smog front soaring, 142

Thermaling, 43, 133
Thermaling, over cities, 60
Thermaling, dry, 47
Thunderstorm flying, 43, 50–51, 134, 136–140
Tight spiraling, 47
Touring by sailplane, 48
Wave soaring, 110 ff., 122–123, 128 ff., 137
Spalding, Reuben Jasper, 8; *ill.,* 10
Steinmetz, Charles Proteus, 11–12; *ill.,* 13
Symonds, Bob, 112–115

**T**

Treese, Hetty, 140
Twining, Prof. Harry La Verne, 29–31; *ill.,* 29

**U**

Ursinius, Oskar, 34

**V**

Voisin, Gabriel, 33, 53
Von Karman, Prof. Theodore, 33–34
Von Loessl, Eugene, 34

**W**

Whitehead, Gustave, 5
Wingate, Gen. Orde, 105
Winkler, Thomas J., Sr., 127
Wright brothers, 5, 6, 16, 19 ff., 35, 37, 53; *ill.,* 21, 22

# RECOMMENDED READING

The following books are available from
Schweizer Aircraft Corp., Box 147, Elmira, New York 14902:
HOW TO GET STARTED IN SOARING
SOARING FOR DIAMONDS by Joseph C. Lincoln
WHERE NO BIRDS FLY by Philip Wills
THE STORY OF GLIDING by Ann and Lorne Welch
METEOROLOGY FOR GLIDER PILOTS by C. E. Wallington
GO GLIDING by Welch and Denes

The following books are available from
Soaring Society of America, Box 66071, Los Angeles, California 90066:
THE JOY OF SOARING by Carle Conway
THE THEORY OF MODERN CROSS-COUNTRY SOARING
by Fred Weinholtz
WITHOUT VISIBLE MEANS OF SUPPORT by Richard N. Miller
AMERICAN SOARING HANDBOOK edited by Alice Fuchs

## A NOTE ABOUT THE AUTHOR

As a high school student in Hollywood, California, Don Dwiggins built the wing of a primary glider in a hallway of the family home. He had to dismantle it to get it out, but that didn't stop him from going to a nearby soaring site at Palos Verde Hills for advice from such experts as Charles Lindbergh and Hawley Bowlus.

Following his enlistment with the Glider Corps in World War II, Mr. Dwiggins became Aviation Editor of the *Los Angeles Daily News,* and for a feature story once rode the awesome Sierra Wave with veteran birdman Harland Ross.

A licensed glider pilot, as well as a commercial power plane flight instructor, Mr. Dwiggins is the author of more than fifteen aviation books and several hundred magazine articles on flying. He is currently Western Regional Director of the Aviation/Space Writers Association. In 1968, he won the AWA best book writing award for his biography of the late movie stunt pilot, Paul Mantz, called *Hollywood Pilot. On Silent Wings* is his third book in Grosset & Dunlap's Adventures In Flight series. The others he wrote are *The Barnstormers* and *Famous Flyers and the Ships They Flew.*